THE SLOG SMUGGLERS

A Boarder's-eye view of Steyning Grammar School in the 1950s

George Barker

GEORGE BARKER
Chapel St
Warmington
Peterborough PE8 6TR

THE SLOG SMUGGLERS

ISBN 0-9540342-0-1

First Published March 2001 by
GEORGE BARKER
Chapel St
Warmington
Peterborough PE8 6TR

Printed in Great Britain By Unity Print Ltd

In memory of all the staff and boys of
Steyning Grammar School in the 1950s no longer with us,
and for the enjoyment of those who survive.

Mr Jones

Twenty years have gone and more
Since I went knocking at the door
Of Mr Jones my housemaster.

Ten to nine, the fatal time
And climbed the stair with creaky tread
In fear and trembling and awful dread
Of that which lay in store.

Now what is he to me? A memory
That taught me mathematics with a glee
And enthusiasm inherent in the Welshman
That he was.

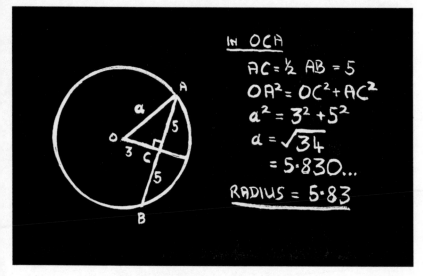

In OCA

$AC = \frac{1}{2} AB = 5$

$OA^2 = OC^2 + AC^2$

$a^2 = 3^2 + 5^2$

$a = \sqrt{34}$

$\quad = 5.830...$

RADIUS = 5.83

The circle he drew upon the board
Was near in his mind to God
In its perfect execution.

He lives on in me does Mr Jones
An image as clear as though this were the year
When his nasal tone first droned
Those nimble figures into my head.

Contents

Foreword

On 3 August 2000 I went into the old Grammar School buildings again for the first time in forty years. The Lower School Secretary, Mrs Ford-Dunn, and I spent four hours walking through classrooms, dormitories, gardens and playgrounds and, as we did so, I talked about some of the things I remembered. As I left, she asked whether I could jot down some of this for the record. Once back at home, I got a sheet of paper and started with a list of two or three word memory-joggers. One memory led to another and the notes then began to expand into sentences, the sentences into paragraphs and the paragraphs into chapters. The thing took over, and I write this foreword two months and fourteen chapters later.

This is not a carefully researched history. It is personal memories, biased and incomplete. It is about life in Holland House, and the day boys get scarcely a mention. To add further personal bias is my interpretation, forty years down the line, of what other people thought and what their objectives were. I may be - I probably am - taking unwarrantable liberties in doing so. It is, in part, in Vicars Bell's words, a rueful rubbing of the backside of my memory, and, in part, a celebration of growing up in the company of a colourful group of young people and adults. I offer apologies in advance to many of those named and especially to David Skippings, whose memory of events will deviate considerably from mine, unless he has changed a great deal since we met last!

It not being a statistical piece of work, readers are dropped in at the deep end - as I was - but it may help to understand that the school held around three hundred and fifty boys, of which about one hundred were boarders. All the boarders were in Holland House. The day boys were split into three Houses, Chancton, Cuthman and Cissa - this last with a soft 'C', please note!

Those anxious for some real history, I would point in the direction of J.M. Sleight's *A Very Exceptional Instance: Three Centuries of Education in Steyning, Sussex* and Stewart Angell's *The Secret Sussex*

1

Resistance - this for an idea of Johnny's war. Anecdotes from former pupils of earlier days are in *Schooldays Remembered. Recollections of Steyning Grammar School 1840-1960.* J.M. Sleight (ed).

My contemporary and friend, David Tas, has kindly allowed me to use one of his poems as a 'frontispiece' to this account, for which permission, much thanks. My sincere thanks to Jean Scragg who corrected the glaring errors of fact made in the first draft, made many helpful suggestions and helped me and many others before and after me to launch ourselves into the flood of a Grammar School boarding house without capsizing.

George Barker.
8 Chapel Street,
Warmington,
Peterborough
PE8 6TR
September 2000

Prologue

Our car was a 1930s, black, four-door Austin saloon, complete with running-board, a large boot and with enough room for four children on the back seat. One early September afternoon in 1951 I, my trunk, tuck-box and overnight case were loaded into it, and driven by my mother the thirty miles across West Sussex from Rogate to Steyning. Parking in Church Street, we unloaded and, for the first of two times in an eight year period, I went into Steyning Grammar School through the staff entrance, to wait in the small entrance hall. I remember that Matron and Nurse were on hand to greet us and show where things went, and being taken up to Long Dorm to find my bed.

I was a veteran of boarding schools myself, having spent a year at one when I was eight or nine. I was surprised now to find a couple of boys in tears as their parents left. One of my new companions though was bright and cheerful, coming over with a smile:

"My name is Michael," he said, "what is yours?"

My name is Michael. What is yours?

3

"Barker!" was my repressive reply. One thing that my previous school had taught me was that everyone was called by their surnames. Mike McNiff never forgot this exchange, but, I hasten to say, we went about together a good deal from then on.

I suppose that someone made sure that we knew what to do when bells rang to signal tea, and showed us where to sit. New boys had a table to themselves. There were two other larger tables with benches for the intermediates and seniors, and there was a small table with chairs at the foot of the room for the prefects. There were about 90 boys all told. A staff table was at the top of the room with chairs, a table cloth, proper china, tea in a pot - milk and sugar separate - thin bread and butter, jam and a plate of cakes. We had none of these!

After about twenty minutes of hectic eating, the duty master banged a gavel and there was silence. He produced a sheet of paper and began briskly:

"Allen?"

"Yes, sir."

"Bacon?"

"Yes, sir."

"Ballard?"

"Yes, sir."

"Barker?"

Silence.

"Barker?"

Still silence.

"Is there a new boy here called Barker? If so, please stand up."

I stood, with difficulty since the bench was in the way.

"Boy, when your name is called in roll call you say "Yes, sir". Do you understand?"

"Yes, sir."

"Good!"

"Barker?"

"Yes, sir."

That is one of the disadvantages of being at the top of alphabetical lists. At least my companions now knew what to do when their names

4

were called. Every year it was the same. Every year too the old sweats took malicious pleasure in listening for new names which sounded strange or amusing to them. McNiff did not pass unremarked, of course, but the main concern about mine was whether I was related to a day-boy School Prefect called Barker. Mercifully, I was not.

The inhabitants of Long Dorm had their washing and changing room up a steep flight of stairs at the Big School end of the dormitory. Here were a toilet cubicle, two bath cubicles, a lead-lined deep shower - which worked spasmodically - and about ten round sinks with taps around the walls of the room. At the same level, and leading off it, was Upper Dorm which, alas, housed half-a-dozen boys a year older than us, who were adept at making rat's-tails out of towels and flicking smaller boys most painfully with them - until, that is, the smaller boys got the trick of it too and fought back - and a small room overlooking Church Street which housed the boarding-house Captain, Dave Hurry. No-one argued with Hurry and his six-foot-six presence in the area guaranteed that our torments were relatively few.

That first night, once we had been driven into bed, the bed areas were inspected by the dormitory captain, Michael Finch. It was part of our learning process. We found that our clothes were supposed to be folded and on the chair at the foot of the bed; that our bed-side lockers must not hold edible things; and that our damp towels should be hung over the head of the bed. The beds themselves were metal framed, with wire lattice springs and flock mattresses. Each had a standard issue of a couple of blankets, and among the kit we had to bring was a rug to supplement these. It was normally kept folded at the foot of the bed. We also provided sheets and pillowcases. Beds were allocated by Matron and there was no lively hope that any appeal would succeed to change your bed with someone, so you could not arrange to be close to friends.

After lights-out, Finch walked slowly up and down Long Dorm, telling exactly what was expected of us, what to do at any given signal, how to address different people, and what we must not do. I can hear, in my mind, the slow pacing, leather heels on creaking floor-

5

boards, and the measured phrases. It was a considerate thing to do. As dormitory captain to the new boys it was his first real taste of responsibility and he was probably as nervous as we were. Even fifty years on, I am still grateful to him for his care and effort. Parts stay in my mind.

"You will find it all strange to begin with. I will try to tell you what will happen between now and this time tomorrow. You won't remember it all and will have to ask if you don't know what to do. I will help as much as I can, but, as I have things to do myself, you won't always find me.

"After lights-out, you are not allowed to talk, play games, read or anything like that. You go to sleep. You are not allowed to get up before the rising bell at half-past-seven, except to go to the toilet. You do not have to get permission to go to the toilet, so I don't want anyone waking me up to ask!

"When you hear the rising bell you get up, go upstairs to wash, come back and dress. Then make your beds. Fold your pyjamas and put them under your pillow. Straighten your locker and chair and then ask me to inspect everything. You can then go into the playground if

A prefect will inspect your...

you want to. You are not allowed back into the dormitory without permission until bed-time.

"At ten to eight, there is the first bell for breakfast. It is only a warning bell and you are not allowed into the dining hall until the second bell at five to eight. You go into the dining hall down the stairs by Big School. The entrance from the staff hall is used only by staff and prefects. Do not sit down, but line up by the table with your backs to it. A prefect will inspect your hands, hair and shoes and if they don't

6

pass you will be sent out to put things right. If you are sent out, you report to the prefect when you come back.

"After breakfast, there is about half-an-hour before Assembly. You can go to the Common Room to read the paper or play in the playground. The day boys turn up and at five to nine the bell goes for Assembly in the gym. You line up in forms across the gym with 2B right in front of the stage and 2A behind 2B. There will be prefects there to show you.

"After prayers, you go to your classes. Look at the timetable on the Big School landing to see where you are. Ask if you don't know where a classroom is, because you will change rooms each period. Make sure you have all your books for the periods until the next break.

"There are two dinners in the dining hall. Boarders' dinner is first, right after the last morning period. Day-boys dinner is later. Don't go to the wrong one! After dinner, boarders go to Big School for Names. A prefect reads the House list and you tell him where you are going after school and who with. For the first few days you will be told what to do after school, but soon you will have to make your own plans.

"Tea is at half-past-five - first bell at twenty-five past. You have another inspection. After tea, when term gets going, you go to Big School for prep until seven when there are Prayers. After Prayers there is cocoa in the dining hall and then second prep. You come out at quarter-past-eight. Change, wash, and read or talk until lights-out at quarter to nine.

"You'll see a bath rota pinned up by the baths. See what day you are down for. If you are down for First Baths, you have to ask to come out of prep at eight. You must be out of the bath by quarter-past so Second Baths can use them. After your bath, put on your dressing gown and slippers and knock on Matron's door. She will inspect you.

"That's more than enough for now. I'll tell you some of this again, and other things as they come up. Come to see me if you get stuck. That's what I'm here for.

"As I said, you'll find it strange at first. I know I did. I like it here now and expect you will too when you're used to it."

There was a slightly stunned pause and then a small voice from out of the dark:

"Please, Finch?"

7

"Yes?"

"Thank you!"

"OK," rather embarrassed, I expect, "Go to sleep! Good night!"

On the whole, those in authority were pretty kind to the new boys for the first week or so. During that first term too, Mrs Scragg, the Headmaster's wife, invited us to tea once a week, and read us in instalments the whole of *The Happy Return*, which we all enjoyed and which introduced me to Horatio Hornblower, whose company I still seek occasionally. It gave us a chance to see our Headmaster - if fleetingly, because he kept in the background on these visits - in a domestic setting, and it gave Mrs Scragg a chance to assess how we were settling in and whether anyone seemed to be in difficulties. I liked that little touch of home and was grateful for it.

It *was* strange. Sometimes it was frightening. It could be uncomfortable - even miserable. Boarders, away from home for the first time, suffered the pangs of home-sickness and muffled sobbing after lights-out was not rare. However, boarders *had* to get on with one-another. They formed a tight-knit community within the larger community of the school. 'Day bugs' were tolerated, some of our friends were, indeed, 'day bugs', but they were definitely an inferior class of being. Any older 'day bug' found pushing a boarder around was asking to bring down upon himself a stinging swarm of that boarder's contemporaries and, if he was not careful, or if he persisted, the full might of Holland House's wrath:

"Please, Hurry! The day bugs are pushing McNiff around in the playground!"

"Are they? We'll soon stop that!"

I was lucky. Quite serious bullying had been rife before I arrived. One or two instances brought matters to a head - a young boy was quite badly hurt, for example, after being put into a laundry basket and rolled down the stairs from Big School landing.

The staff and senior prefects combined in a concerted attempt to stamp out bullying of junior boys by seniors. I remember being picked up in one hand by a VI Former and being banged against a class-mate held in his other. This was on Big School landing and was interrupted only when

8

Chris Potter, a Holland House School Prefect, came hurtling down the stairs from Dave Hurry's room and saw what was going on. We juniors were swept aside, the VI Former propelled into Big School, and the door banged shut. There was a murmur of voices and a couple of sharp cracks. The door flew open and Chris passed by upon his lawful occasions, with only a brief glance at us to reassure himself we were in one piece. The VI Former emerged unsteadily, dazed and bruised.

Although psychologists might disapprove of meeting fire with fire in this way, it worked when persuasion had failed. Chris was then Southern Area schools heavyweight boxing champion and was short of volunteers for sparring. Any boy large enough, and caught bullying, was passed on to the games master as fit for the purpose.

The anti-bullying campaign needed the authority and lead given by the staff. However, the authority of the staff paled to insignificance beside that of the Holland House Prefects. These seemed to be with you always - even unto the ends of the earth! They had the power to make life not worth living, and they knew what was going on in a way the staff did not. The alliance of staff and prefects saw the worst kinds of bullying banished. Something which had been normal, if not actually fashionable previously, was now looked down on.

Having said that, lower grade bullying - boys from a year or two above tormenting those in the years beneath - did go on. However, the close knit community of boarders helped to make sure that things did not get out of hand, and the first signs of real distress usually brought the cry: "OK! Leave him alone! He's had enough".

All in all, we were a pretty cheerful bunch and got on reasonably well with one another, but the community of boys played out its role against a backdrop of buildings, each with its own distinctive character, and a supporting cast of school staff, many of whom were most certainly characters.

The Prologue is over. Bring on the Players!

Chapter 1

Teachers and other staff

In the early 1950s, there were seventeen teachers, eighteen counting the visiting chaplain. They were a combination of those who had taught there throughout the war, those who had been in the Services and returned to teaching or trained as teachers once de-mobbed, and some of the first crop of people graduating without having been in the Services, other than for the compulsory eighteen months National Service. The sudden availability of teachers after the war, gave the Headmaster and Governors a good choice of people and by 1951 there were few poor teachers at the school. All but one, Freda Sage, until 1953 the art mistress, were male.

Almost all had nick-names - never used to their faces, but normal in any discussion about them by the boys. Most were pretty obvious. The Headmaster was known as 'Johnny' because he always signed himself 'John Scragg'; Mr Jones, the formidable senior maths master and Holland Housemaster, was 'Jonah'; the woodwork master, Mr James, was 'Jamie'. The junior biology master and resident master in Coombe Court, John Luker, was known throughout his career as 'Joe'.

Initials played a part in others: 'Top' (T.O. Prethero), the Chancton Housemaster; 'Percy' Coltman the senior English master (P.C. Coltman); 'Ike' Williams the senior biology master (I.K. Williams); 'Pog' Sauvain the geography master and resident master in Dormer in the late-1950s (P.O.G. Sauvain). The combination of his surname and an enthusiasm for archaeological excavation dictated that Bill Gardener, the Latin master and resident master in Wykeham, was called 'Digger'.

Some names derived from shape or demeanour, so we had: 'Spud' Crannigan, a short, spherical junior French and English master, resident in No 7; 'Flab' Wright, the bow-tied Andrew Flintoff of the Staff and the Steyning cricket teams; 'Slopey Joe' Baker, who carried one shoulder higher than the other, another French master who played the piano for assembly, and took singing lessons; 'Drip' Walters, the geography master and resident master in Dormer from about 1952 until the mid-1950s, because he looked a bit of a drip - although he was not - and because 'Walters' is not far off 'water', at least not to the schoolboy mind; 'Buffer' Bennett, deputy Headmaster, senior chemistry master and Cissa Housemaster, because with his grey hair, moustache and general air of tweedy benevolence he looked like everyone's grandfather.

A couple were more mysteriously named - until you got to know them. 'Glubbie' Gooderson, Jonah's replacement in about 1954 as Holland Housemaster and senior maths master, whose ever-present pipe bubbled and gurgled happily as he drew on it, and 'Shocker' Webster, the games and PE teacher, who addressed all and sundry as 'you shockers'.

A little strangely, perhaps, three of the most popular and respected masters had no nickname so far as I know. These were Keith Sorrell, senior French master and Cuthman Housemaster; Arthur Lee, the dynamic senior history master; and the physics master Mr Blackaby who was always called just 'Mr Blackaby'.

Teachers wore gowns in school hours, although these were replaced with lab coats when in the laboratories or the woodwork and art rooms. For special occasions, such as Speech Day, hoods would be worn. The exception to the rule was Shocker, who always wore a track-suit over singlet and shorts. Even by the standards of the day, it was felt a bit too formal to conduct PE lessons in an academic gown! The visiting chaplain didn't wear a gown either. He was Mr Mackenzie, rector of Storrington. For reasons not known to us, Johnny disapproved of the vicar of Steyning, Mr Egerton-Williams, and so 'Eggie Bill' was never appointed to the post.

It was Mac the chaplain who we could catch out, invariably, by staring intently at his fly-buttons (and they *were* buttons in those days, not zips) as he sat, legs apart, on the edge of the sturdy table on the Big School dais. After a few minutes of stares, grins and surreptitious nudges his nerve always failed and he had to get down, turn round to write on the blackboard - and take a swift and furtive look down. He must have known he was being 'had' but he was never prepared to take the risk!

We tried the same trick once, and once only, with Arthur Lee. He simply looked down and then up at us: "What are you all staring for? There's nothing hanging out!"

No-one would have dreamt even *thinking* of trying it on Jonah.

In fact you took few liberties, although most masters were amiable enough.

The resident masters were in a particularly powerful position so far as the boarders were concerned. Jonah, who could bring the whole school to a state of respectful silence with a glance, terrified junior boarders. The words: "We will see the boy Barker in our study at ten-to-nine", spoken to the House at the end of breakfast, were the black cap of the domestic judicial system. All that remained was to discover, painfully, where on the scale of one stroke to six strokes of the cane the crime in which you had been detected sat. You rarely wished to sit anywhere yourself after a ten-to-nine visit to Jonah. Should, by mischance, PE happen to follow any time that same morning, the evidence was clearly visible to all in the showers afterwards and often brought the cheerful query from Shocker: "Been having a friendly chat with Mr Jones, have you?"

In the classroom, Jonah had the awe-inspiring ability to draw, freehand, perfect circles and straight lines on the blackboard - something in which, you sensed, he took pride. However, he also had the mind-numbing habit, having set you some calculation to do, algebraic formula to solve, or geometric proof to make, of advancing upon you as you stood giving of your poor best to the class, and cuffing the back of your head encouragingly while saying: "Think, boy! Think!" Not easy!

Head cuffing also took place whenever Jonah detected actual or suspected minor misdemeanours. This was invariably accompanied by the half-whispered, slightly sibilant and Welsh-accented: "What is this, boy? What is this?", which everyone in Holland House could imitate. I received this greeting on many occasions - when watching the first 'Slinky' make its way down the stairs in Dormer; throwing

What is this, boy? What is this?

paper darts in Lower Corridor; playing 'chop-sticks' on the piano in Dormer; playing with a stag-beetle on my desk in prep; and, most awful of all, as I was imitating him to one of my friends, cuffing him and saying "What is this, boy? What is this?" when a hand began striking the back of *my* head and I found I had acquired an echo!

Jonah had a daughter, I guess she was in her mid-twenties, who came to live with him when Wykeham Cottage was set up as a house for the Holland Housemaster. Jonah was fairly portly and his daughter had inherited this, but, in addition, carried, as they say, all before her. She was known as 'The Brabazon', or 'Brab' for short, after the Bristol Brabazon, the largest aircraft built in Britain and which we saw on test flights along the south coast. Even with six engines, it was under-powered and always flew tail down, giving the appearance of leaning forward as it moved. Jonah knew of this nickname and it amused him. When her boy-friend arrived to take her out on his motor-bike (poor machine!), we sometimes caught Jonah's cry of: "Brabazon! Your carriage waits you at the door!"

Anyway, back to maths.

Maths exercise books had grey covers, and the sight of a grey-covered note-book still makes my stomach churn. I was *not* good at maths and my distinction in this was shared certainly by two of my class-mates. There was a terrible ceremony and inevitability about the return of maths prep books. In would come Jonah, carrying thirty-three exercise books on top of his register. Someone would be deputed to hand them back to their owners. The register would be opened, half-moon glasses donned, and a silver propelling pencil run down the column of marks. Then: "Stand up the boy Barker .... stand up the boy King .... stand up the boy Lenthall" (always pronounced by him 'Lentall'). A significant pause during which a cold stare was given to us; register snapped shut: "ZERO for our maths prep! We will stay in after school on Thursday!"

In the detention period, more sums were set and at intervals Jonah would visit his reluctant mathematicians to render personal assistance, not to say encouragement. Alas!

I recall one horrendous calculation about a bath of given dimensions, into which water was running at a certain rate from a tap and, because the fool of a compiler of sums had not put the plug into the plug-hole, was simultaneously running out at a different rate. The relationship between the two seemed at one and the same time both improbable and, arithmetically, quite unnecessarily complicated. The question being asked was, how long would it take to fill the bath. Although one toyed with suggesting that it would not take long if you located and inserted the plug, thoughts of studies and ten-to-nine encouraged a more orthodox approach.

After some fifteen ink-splattered minutes, came the re-entry of Jonah: "Let us see, boy! Uh.....Eh!! At this rate, boy, the bath will take all eternity to fill! Where is the error?"

I hazarded a guess at the decimal point. "Yes! Yes! Let us try again."

Again an inky, uncomprehending struggle and then: "Let us see again, boy. Uh.....Eh!!! What are we using to fill the bath with, boy? Yes, a tap! We are not using the Niagara Falls."

And so, Glubbie inherited a mathematician whose mind froze at the sight of grey exercise books and Room 5 (the main maths classroom). However, to our mutual surprise and delight, I managed, just, to scrape a 'pass' at 'O' Level. The following term, as I was standing outside Coombe Court comparing notes with contemporaries, most of whom seemed to have passed maths with top grades, up rushed Glubbie, pink with pleasure and excitement, totally ignoring the mathematical genii and making straight for me: "*Congratulations* laddie! You *passed* laddie! You ***passed***!", and shook my hand as though I were the village pump.

I wasn't very good at physics either, and Mr Blackaby invited me and others on several occasions to join him after school in the physics laboratory. This was almost worth striving for. He always devised practical experiments which would further explain and clarify the problems we had stumbled over, and took great pains to try to get us to understand things properly. It was stimulating and gave us virtually one-to-one teaching.

Jamie's kingdom was the woodwork room. Here, in my first year, he taught me to care for tools and to respect wood. However, for all his patience, my total output was a small box which gave the appearance of having fought the good fight - and lost. I can hear in my mind his voice, in which horror and sadness were blended, saying: "Oh, lad! What have you *done*? You've *r-r-ruined* the wood!"

Oh, lad! What have you done?

Only when disappointment turned into resignation was his ultimate sanction applied: "Lad! Take it over there and spoke-shave it until the bell!"

Others he fashioned into excellent craftsmen (whose products gleamed at Speech Day, the envy of all) but not me. After one year, we agreed that my talents lay more in art than in woodwork. Since art and woodwork went in tandem, with half the class going to the art room while half went into woodwork, changing round halfway through the double period, or with groups alternating weekly, it was possible to opt for one or the other. Jamie, I am sure, took the view that inept carpenters could do themselves, and others, more damage than inept artists - after seeing my class-mate Jimmy Binns in action I would share his sentiments - and he made sure that Miss Sage, and subsequently Mr Alabone, took the more highly challenged of his potential master-carpenters at the earliest opportunity.

I cannot think that my artistic efforts were better than very average, but I enjoyed splashing the paint (mixed from powder and water) about, and the mental stimulus of choosing which bit to illustrate from the graphic account of something read out to us.

I recall, in my first year, the occasion Freda Sage posed for us (fully clad, I hasten to add - none of this modern nonsense about nude models in your 1950s Grammar Schools!). I happened to catch a glimpse of her through the door, looking at our efforts. Her face was screwed up and she was making a funny mewing noise. I am still uncertain whether she was laughing or crying!

Her pinnacle of fame in the school was reached when a gathering of some formality somewhere in Brighton, and involving the great and the good of the area, was reported, in part, by the *Evening Argus* thus: ".....Also present was the Headmaster of Steyning Grammar School, Mr John Scragg, with one of his mistresses".

The staff collected several copies (this was years before photocopiers became available) and so were able to ensure that the cutting was replaced sufficiently frequently on the school notice-board in Upper Corridor every time that Johnny removed it, to let most of the school enjoy it.

Although nude models were denied us, in fact they were available in Steyning. This we discovered when Arthur Lee, who dabbled in painting, decided to get Johnny's goat by renting space in an upstairs room in the Norfolk Arms to use as a studio. It was virtually opposite Johnny's own bedroom in Holland Cottage. Arthur then hired a female model and worked in the evenings after dark, with the light full on and the curtains pulled back. I do not know whether Johnny rose to the bait. The local police, however, did. The room was also visible from School Lane, and the police observed that the interest in human anatomy being shown by the boys made it virtually impossible for anyone to walk past Dormer because of the wall-to-wall lust-jam.

Arthur Lee was entertaining in his classes too. He was a good and energetic teacher, who delighted in encouraging and expressing unorthodox views. A great believer in saying what you really thought instead of what you felt society expected you to say, he encouraged us to do the same. His politics lay left of centre, but perhaps not so far left as his assumption of communism (complete with red tie) suggested. The school 'establishment' was True Blue, and Arthur always enjoyed spicing things up.

Over the five years to 'O' Levels, we graduated from the pyramids and shadoofs of ancient Egypt to Walpole and Pitt, with occasional forays into modern politics to add variety. In teaching us to think (and several other of the staff did this too), he also recognised the need to serve examiners with orthodoxy, however incorrect, in preference to an unfamiliar re-interpretation of the facts, however correct. In 'O' Level year we were handed a series of 'model' essays which he had written and which covered the main items in that year's curriculum. "If you learn that lot by heart you are guaranteed a good pass," we were told, with the inevitable rider: "A lot of it is rubbish, but it is what they want."

His job that year, he explained, was to teach us to pass exams rather than to explore history. His final advice before the exam was cast in the form of a promise to castrate, personally, anyone attempting to answer any question outside the period we had been covering, however tempting: "Your vague memories of first year lessons on shadoofs do not make you an Egyptologist knowing all about agricultural irrigation systems. You *do* know about Walpole's policies, however boring and stupid you find them and you'll bloody well write about them. I've got bets on your results and if you ruin my prospects I'll ruin yours! Good luck!"

Poor choice of questions was not the only potential pitfall in exams. In 'O' Level biology, one of my contemporaries, Woggie Skelton, wrote an erudite account of the functions of the kidney in response to the examiners' invitation to describe the functions of the liver. He passed, but probably dropped a grade. The mistake came from wishful thinking. He had 'revised' the kidney the evening before!

Other fond memories of Arthur Lee include his revolt against a school dinner in which mince was for first course and rice pudding for second. He swept in, a little late, marching briskly up on the serving-hatch side towards the staff table at the far end. He took in the mince being served and then the rice lurking on hot-plates in the kitchen. Without changing expression or slackening pace he marched behind the staff table, down the window side of the hall, out of the doors and into School Lane, heading, no doubt, to the Norfolk Arms for bread, cheese, pickles and beer.

Although a rumbustious member of any staff team got up to play the School First Elevens in cricket, hockey or football, Arthur saw no reason to buy special kit to grace the occasion. A pair of army shorts, long khaki socks, and a pair of brown-painted Service hob-nailed boots did for hockey and football. An old pair of grey flannels and the same hob-nailed boots, whitened in deference to convention, served for cricket. All were played with extreme ferocity and God help your shins if either Arthur's hobnails (football - usually!) or hockey stick met them.

Arthur played with great ferocity...

Another inspiring teacher was Percy Coltman, the senior English master. He did not tolerate slip-shod work, or laziness. His standards were high and became more demanding as you rose up the school. He taught us correct use of words and grammar and, if we cared to pay attention, how to send words out to work for us. I dread to think what he would make of my writing now! I know that one of my contemporaries, who still writes and publishes poetry, credits Percy for anything he has achieved. To this debt I would add the gift of teaching me how to analyse a book in detail and to look in depth at what an author has written.

He had to suffer our poor grammar and experimental spelling. In periods where we read out loud, taking it in turn down the rows in the class, he also had to suffer our mispronunciations. When you are an enthusiastic, young reader - as most of us were in our spare time - occasionally, you hear in your mind, pronunciation of a word which is not that given to it by the majority of the population. If it is not a word you use frequently in conversation, that mistake becomes embedded. So it was that my best friend, Dai Tas, putting heart and soul into the accusation: 'You have misled the king!', pronounced it 'mizzelled', to the joy of the class. Shortly afterwards, I went one better and, in a descriptive piece, read to my delighted audience that: 'In the evening, the soldiers were sitting around, warming their hands on the brassières...', instead of 'braziers'. Once the class had picked itself up, Percy remarked that, while what I had said might well have been so, soldiers being what they are, it was not what was written. This set everyone off again, as he had intended. No-one, myself included, would call a brazier anything other than a brazier in future.

Ironically, I did some of my best work for him anonymously. A boy a year older than I and who I knew because our homes were near to one another, was in the English VI Form when I was in Remove. They were learning about different forms of verse and, each week, were given the task of producing their own example of a sonnet, a piece of satire, or whatever was on the class menu. Although good at English, he had a bit of a blind spot for rhythm, rhyme and different metres. He found that, by explaining to me just what was wanted in

20

terms of content, length, style and metre, I could produce the goods for him. He would copy what I had written and hand it in. It lasted just one term, but only once did he (I) get less than 9/10. It was reduced to 7/10 once because of a dubious emphasis in one word to get the metre right! Never in my school career did I get such consistently high marks on my own account. Not for anything!

I found English enjoyable, but not Latin. This surprises me now because, in coping with the English lexicon, I would not be without the information drummed into me by Digger, and wish now that I had paid a bit more attention and that the school had done Greek too. I associate Latin periods with a classroom in the now defunct Coombe Court building. It had been the dining room or living room in the earlier life of the building and thirty people made for a tight fit. Here we construed Virgil and learnt declensions.

Given the chance of choosing for 'O' Level between taking geography (which I liked and was good at) or Latin (which I didn't and wasn't), I leapt at the geography option. Digger and I parted company with mutual sighs of relief. At the end of the Christmas term my report arrived at home and there was an unparalleled scene. In order to gain admission either to Oxford or to Cambridge, certain passes at 'O' Level were mandatory. Maths and English were two. Latin was a third. The reason was simple. A hundred years before, lectures at both universities - and, indeed at most universities across Europe - were given in Latin. An advantage, of course, was that you could tour the leading universities, hearing the most famous professors, with no language barrier to make life difficult. That this was no longer the case, was neither here nor there to the university admissions boards. While a week is a long time in politics, a hundred years in the sight of Oxbridge, like a thousand ages in the sight of the Lord, are like an evening gone. Indeed, when I eventually got to Oxford, the zoology syllabus was still that set down by Ray Lankester in about 1860.

At all events, after a series of brief exchanges, wreathed with the smoke of battle, between parents and school, Digger and I found ourselves in each other's company once more.

Having spent a term studying glaciation instead of Virgil, I was behind everyone else, and once or twice a week Digger and I performed a reluctant duet after school in an attempt to get me up to speed. It had been decided that I would do two set books - the rest did only Virgil, but had a 'difficult' unseen as well - and so these extra sessions were often spent in the company of Julius Caesar. Essential equipment for any schoolboy doing Latin were the cribs. We were encouraged to use them in fact. Some were a bit of a challenge in themselves. What, for example, is a fifteen-year-old to make of: "Just as when at times with chinky thunder-bursts the lightning leaps athwart the skies..." and I remember Digger's pen firmly deleting "For despatch of lading..." from the Caesar crib and substituting "For speed in loading...".

Although I failed in my first attempt, a second, made solo a term later and demanding a trip to a church hall somewhere in Brighton to sit the exam, saw me pass with a higher grade either than I (or Digger) had expected, or that I deserved.

Digger came into his own at end-of-term jollifications. In class we were quite likely to be taught to sing 'Ego sum testudo, atque hoc superbio' or other ditties in Latin. On stage he was a good actor, and I remember a virtuoso performance when he had to stand in as Mrs Malaprop in the school play at twenty-four hours notice. His mime, given at a Christmas revue, of his Headmaster going fishing, is a lasting memory too. Johnny got his revenge by requiring Digger to teach the whole school to sing a hymn in Latin for the Founder's Day service.

He also ran the Archaeological Society and in 1951 was well into the excavation, in which boys of all ages were able to take part, of a round barrow on Steyning Round Hill. Unfortunately, in 1952 or 1953, the Estate ploughed up the downland and bull-dozed the excavation without warning. The school buzzed with fury and Digger penned a lament which was posted on the school noticeboard. Only a few lines come back to me now, but it began:

"With pick and spade we climbed aloft
Across the Round Hill of Steyning's verdure soft..."and ended:

"No more is our belovéd mound atop the ridge.
Site fit henceforth only for pilgrimage."
Hardly deathless verse, but heart-felt!

All the school had regular PE lessons in the gym. This was the personal domain of Shocker Webster who worked everyone pretty hard and drilled us as though we were platoons of soldiers:

"AttenTION!! Stand up *straight*! Shoulders *back*! Chests *out*!"

A pause while he prowled up and down the rows: "Pull your stomach in, boy."

Then: "Right, you shockers! Circuit training today. Apparatus out at the word 'go'. GO!"

In the initial set of warming up exercises - arm and knee bends, torso twists, and so on - he often sent the whole class jogging round the gym, while he stood to one side idly swinging in his hand the thin nylon ropes used to run out and hoist the beam. Anyone running sloppily was liable to get a painful flick as they went by.

The wall-bars were an especial means of torture. Hanging from the top bar with your legs held straight and horizontally in front of you while he walked slowly round leering at straining faces, may have been excellent for stomach muscles, but was agony at the time.

Safety was of paramount importance, although we were encouraged to 'have a go' at quite difficult vaults. For every vaulter there had to be one or two people 'standing in', ready to field and break a fall if necessary. For the trickier stuff, Shocker 'stood in' himself and some of the less proficient were not allowed to try the vault. For the easier ones, the class streamed over in succession with each boy, having done his jump, standing in for the one following. Thus it was that I was 'standing in' for Andy Treacher in the gate-vault over the beams when his foot got mixed up with the waist-band of my gym shorts. At that stage in our innocence and youth we wore nothing under our shorts for support. I was, therefore, stripped quite bare in the twinkling of an eye. It took a good deal of frantic scrabbling amongst the tightly rolled-up shorts, which now pinned my ankles together, before my modesty could be restored. Shocker was crying with laughter and my heartless classmates, given his lead, excelled themselves. It is odd that I found it embarrassing, since only a few minutes later the entire class would be scampering around naked, getting a shower before going to the next period. I think it was the total unexpectedness, and the rapidity with which disaster struck, which startled me - the gale of laughter wasn't much of a help either.

I was stripped quite bare in the twinkling of an eye....

Shocker often demonstrated what he wanted. If this was done with pre-planning on his part, he would take off his tracksuit. If, however, the demonstration was impromptu - to correct an error someone had made, for example - he would not take the time to strip off, but simply call a halt and then do it. I remember well the consequent cascade of keys, coins, penknife, confiscated marbles, toffees and other items, if the demonstration involved standing on the hands or any other such manoeuvre which allowed the laws of gravity full rein on the contents of his pockets.

In some ways, one of the masters we most underestimated, certainly at first, was Slopey Joe Baker. His principal subject was French, mainly with the juniors, but being quite a good pianist and interested in music he usually played the piano for Assembly and the boarders' evening and Sunday services - although when any of the boys were considered good enough, they too contributed. Naturally, he drew the short straw to take the singing periods with the juniors and without a flicker of a smile, but with a grim fortitude, endured tortured renderings of 'Drink to me only with thine eyes', 'Danny boy', 'By yon bonny banks and yon bonnie braes' and all the rest of the late Victorian selection of ditties felt suitable for schoolboys. It was not until well after I left that I came across 'I know where I'm going' for the first time and bitterly regret that it was not in the repertoire. To be licensed to sing a verse which runs:

'Some say he's black, but I say he's bonnie;

Fairest of them all, my lovely, winsome Johnny'was a pleasure foregone.

Slopey Joe had under his wing anyone wishing to learn to play the piano. At that time it was piano or bust, so far as musical instruments went, although recorders were making a tentative appearance by the time I left in 1959. There were three pianos in the school: a grand piano in Big School; a grand piano on the stage in the gym; and an upright piano kept in what had, I believe, been a downstairs bathroom or kitchenette in Dormer. This little room could hold the piano and two chairs, but nothing else. The upright was tortured daily by novices. The Big School piano was for the more proficient and the piano in the gym was reserved for experts - although it was usually no more or no less in tune than the Big School one. The upright was in tune with nothing and certainly not with itself.

If anyone wanted to learn another instrument, they were best advised to become a day boy and join the Salvation Army.

Your musical education was not abandoned when advancing years, with their accompanying breaking voices and over-heated imaginations made singing lessons inadvisable especially since their fare of ballads was full of dubious *double entendres* - at least so far as adolescent minds were concerned. The advances in modern technology meant that not only were gramophones being replaced by record players but also that the short and fragile 78 records were being replaced by long playing vinyl discs. Several of the staff had record players and there was a school machine.

Thus in the third year, we found that singing in the gym with Slopey Joe had turned itself into musical appreciation in Big School with Joe Luker. Joe was the junior biology (and chemistry) master and in senior classes dealt with botany. He enjoyed simply listening to music and so was marked down rapidly for this endeavour. He hit on a brilliant ploy. Mussorgsky's 'Pictures at an Exhibition' in the Ravel orchestration was published as an 'Ace of Clubs' LP. The sleeves of this admirable series had quite full notes on them about the pieces and in this case the music represents a series of contrasting pictures, each carefully described in the notes. The piece is in distinct sections - the pictures and promenades - which lent themselves perfectly to a school period. The music itself is classical enough to please fans of traditional classical music, but rumbustious and modern enough to appeal to *aficionados* of other kinds of music. So for one term we dipped weekly into 'Pictures at an Exhibition', ending up triumphantly in the final period putting the whole thing together by listening to it from start to finish for the first time. It still conjures up images of Big School and Joe when I hear it.

Modern technology did not end in the school with record players. Far from it, and Slopey Joe was, as we found to our great discomfort, custodian of a great mystery. He lived in a small flat in the Main School, above the School Secretary's office. One evening he invited a group of boarding VI Formers to his rooms to have tea. We all settled down in one room. He got a conversation going to his satisfaction and, having as it were pointed us in the right direction for his purposes, left to go to make the tea. We chatted on, speculating on his motives in inviting us; touching on the morals, or lack of them, of certain of our acquaintances; and criticising the Headmaster's latest edicts. In the slight pause greeting his return, he put down the tea-pot, said: "Oh! Just let me turn this thing off," and went behind the settee to emerge with a massive tape-recorder which he had persuaded the Powers-That-Be to buy for language classes. We had never seen one before and did not know what it did. In a few excruciatingly embarrassing moments we found out. You have no idea how your whole soul sinks when you know that what you have said behind their back is about to be repeated, faithfully and with no hope of denial, to someone's face. That 'someone' too, was a member of school staff and one with the reputation of being a strict and humourless disciplinarian.

He wound it back, started it up and hell opened wide its doors to half-a-dozen worried young men. After a few desultory remarks, you heard clearly:

"What is Slopey up to? He's up to something, isn't he?"

"Yeah! I reckon so too. I reckon he's..."

At this point he clicked off the sound, wound it back and pressed the 'delete' button saying cheerfully:

"Well, that's enough of that I think, but you get the idea. From now on the walls may indeed have ears!"

The relief was palpable.

The rest of the tea-party was spent speaking at the machine and listening with incredulity to our own voices. I could hardly recognise mine - although everyone else said it sounded just like me. It was the same for us all. It is the same for me now. When I hear a recording of an interview I may have given, my first thought is: "Who is that idiot and what is he blathering on about?"

As I say, Slopey Joe was strict, but we became aware that he was far from humourless, and was concerned for our welfare and progress. Among the juniors it was felt, as a pupil of Dr Temple's once said of him, that he was a beast, but a just beast. He worked to the rules, but applied them absolutely consistently. You knew exactly where you were. There was nothing so despised and feared by us than a master - or prefect - who might one minute let you off for quite serious offences, but, the next, punish severely a minor misdemeanour. The boarders were sorry when he left to better himself at another school and to marry. Everyone contributed to his leaving present and, by our standards, we raised a lot of money. When his gift was given to him, he was clearly surprised at the warmth of the applause, believing himself to be unpopular, and was moved by it. He managed to say little, but included a joke which took us all aback and wafted him out of Big School on a wave of astonished laughter:

"Thank you all very much indeed! And now I suppose there is nothing left for me to do, except just Slope off!"

Someone else who did the unexpected just when we thought we could predict his every move was Buffer Bennett. He had been at the school certainly from the mid-1930s and had taught chemistry solidly and, so far as we could tell, from the same text-books, ever since. He was kindly and unperturbable. He had added to his reputation during the war for carrying on teaching a class in the old library as a bomb going off nearby brought the ceiling down on everyone - at least, that is what we were told, though not by him. The bomb fell on houses in Church Street opposite Chantry Green and rumour had it that it was dropped by a German Old Boy called Reidl who had said, when he left, that he would come back with a bomb.

The chemistry laboratory was the room to the left as you went down Lower Corridor and opposite the rear door into the lab was the chemical store and prep room. The wooden benches had sinks and gas taps at intervals along them and there were bigger sinks and further bench space under the windows looking onto the playground. Beneath the benches were cupboards which held things such as Bunsen burners, tripods, gauze mats, Bunsen tubing and some flasks and beakers. We sat on lab stools - precariously. At the front and rear of the lab and against the outside wall were fume cupboards in which lived, permanently, the Kipps apparatus and, temporarily, any noxious or smelly demonstration preparations. Each bench had sets of bottles of the day-to-day chemicals in constant use - dilute acids and alkalis for example - and 'occasional' chemicals were kept in the prep room or on shelves at the front within easy reach of the teacher. A locked poisons cupboard was also at the front of the lab and at the back was a big cupboard with an assortment of glassware. The chemical balances were on benches along the Lower Corridor walls.

In this setting, chemical mysteries were performed. The standards of safety were pretty low by present-day standards. Our only protection was a lab coat which we provided ourselves. Hands were burned regularly by concentrated acids or by sticks of caustic potash or caustic soda - indeed smokers often put concentrated nitric acid on their fingers to disguise nicotine staining. Beads of mercury, memorials to long-dead thermometers, twinkled merrily from cracks in benches and from between the pieces of the wooden parquet flooring. Gases such as chlorine and hydrogen sulphide were in common use. The only time I recall the lab being closed for safety reasons was when someone dropped a bottle of bromine, the contents of which promptly dived into the crevices in the floor to join the mercury.

However, Buffer was disappointing. He just didn't make mistakes. Even his November 5th lesson about fireworks, held no colourful and unintended explosions. His demonstrations always worked exactly as he said they would. If Buffer, in response to a question, said that in Holmyard, page 272, paragraph 2 lay the answer, on page 272 and in paragraph 2 it did - except when, to our considerable joy, Holmyard was revised by the publishers and Buffer's mind had to be re-programmed in consequence.

We, of course, did our best to compensate for this lack of excitement. Very early on we found that blackboard chalk, stuffed into the end of a piece of Bunsen tubing could be propelled down the lab at huge velocity - but not with Buffer in the room! Similarly, if a Bunsen burner was connected to a water tap, a powerful jet of water was produced which could be directed, fruitfully, at foes. The back bench - where most of the boarders in my class had contrived to congregate - became adept at timing blowing down the gas taps to bring maximum chaos to the experiments of the goodies on the front bench by extinguishing their Bunsen burners. Then there were the personal experiments and unlicensed additions to the authorised mixtures: "Please sir! My solution has gone green and is bubbling!"

Just occasionally Buffer slipped up. In VI Form chemistry he had us all carrying out a test involving a layer of ether through which a pellet of potassium was dropped onto what lay beneath. This was fine, so far as it went; little happened other than the colour change predicted. Test over, the test-tubes were emptied down the sink pipes. Here our experiment encountered the U-tube in which was water. The potassium flared on contact with the water, igniting the ether. In no

Please, Sir! My solution has gone green and is bubbling...

time, explosions were going off all round the lab sending jets of flame erupting from the sinks.

We also discovered that if a syrup tin, with holes punched in the base and the lid, was filled with coal gas and a match applied to the hole in the lid, the result would look like a rather stout candle - until the air flowing in as the gas burned, produced an explosive mixture. The bang was quite satisfying and the lid sometimes reached the ceiling. This was not something to perform while Buffer was in the lab, but the waiting period before his arrival could be enlivened by it. Once, someone had begged from one of the maids a gargantuan tin, which had held school jam. This was filled and lit just as Buffer walked in. He stopped with his back to it and leant against the bench to make some pronouncement - to the agony of the perpetrator who could do nothing to avert calamity while Buffer remained in position. All attempts to move him failed, but, timing it to perfection, Buffer remarked: "Blow it out, boy!" as he walked away. He had known exactly what was going on all the time.

If that was one surprise, it was nothing to that of hearing him use a swear word on two, and only two occasions. You *never* swore in Buffer's hearing. He disapproved entirely. Therefore, when, in an era of adventurous (relatively) haircuts among the day boys, Johnnie Dugnolle shouted across the class "That's a bloody awful haircut Dray!" just as Buffer walked past the open window, the class waited in some trepidation. He walked in. There was silence as everyone stood up. He looked around sternly for the two principals in this and then: "Well, it's a bloody sight better than yours, Dugnolle!"

The second occasion was played to a smaller, but just as appreciative, audience of boys. When he was presiding at boarder's tea one day, sausages had been served and they were not of the usual standard. After he had left the dining hall, the caterer, Mrs Barnes, overheard three or four seniors complaining amongst themselves, rose in her not infrequent wrath, and bundled the lot off with her to find Buffer and to seek retribution.

"Mr Bennett, I want you to punish these boys! I heard them myself say that my sausages were bloody awful sausages!"

Buffer had, however, suffered the sausages too:

"Well, I'm not going to. They *were* bloody awful sausages!"

In spite of his reputation for kindliness and caution, he did manage once to cause Main School to be evacuated. At the time, I was in the biology lab, which was, by then, in Room 3 off Lower Corridor on the right-hand side going down. Outside in the corridor came the sound of breaking glass and, after a brief pause, Buffer's voice saying: "Well, stand away from it!"

Then, almost immediately, dense white 'smoke' billowed up, clearly visible through the biology lab windows and sounds of unrest could be heard from the chemistry lab. Ike Williams, who was teaching us, opened the door to investigate and it turned out that someone had dropped and broken a Winchester bottle of eight-eighty

31

ammonia in the corridor between the prep room and the lab. Buffer had immediately neutralised it by pouring on a Winchester of concentrated hydrochloric acid! The result: a chemical fog of ammonium chloride you could cut with a knife. We were instructed to open the windows and go out into the playground - if we could find it - and not to step in anything.

By this time, Mr James's class in the woodwork room had realised that all was not well. Jamie opened the door and the white fog rolled in there too. The natural draughts of the corridor system carried everything aloft, although in a less concentrated form. Occupants of classrooms off Upper Corridor heard scurrying feet below and voices in the playground where voices should not have been at that time of day. They saw wisps of smoke in the corridor. O Joy Unconfined! The school is burning down! So *they* joined the exodus, disturbing Big School *en route* and emptying that too. Obviously, those in the physics lab were not going to let the opportunity pass them by and gleefully added themselves to the general *mêlée*, together with the erstwhile singers from 2B of 'Nymphs and Shepherds, Come Away' who had been toiling in the gym.

Meanwhile the mighty fog rolled out through doors and windows.

The arrival of Johnny put a dampener on proceedings. His mission was to find out just what and just who were responsible for disturbing the 'noiseless tenor' of his school's ways and, apparently, inciting revolution among the boys. We were commanded, in essence and with threatenings and promises of slaughterings, to: shut up; assemble in class groups; stand still while he investigated; and prepare to confess. At this point arrived the Steyning Fire-Brigade, alerted by locals that the school was on fire.

If Buffer was representative of the staid Old Guard, perhaps I should touch on Flab Wright as a specimen of the new wave of teachers. He arrived in the mid-1950s to replace Slopey Joe. About all he had in common with Buffer was that he parked his car in the small playground at the top of Burdock's Slope. Buffer's car was large, black and square. Flab's was small, open topped and with aluminium body-work curving to a point aft. He was large, with rather floppy ginger hair and a ginger moustache. He wore a bow-tie with 'loud' shirts. He bounced noisily and enthusiastically around the junior forms, and was easily 'red herringed' by the boys into telling anecdotes about university life (or worse), rather than studying French. (If you tried to 'red-herring' Buffer, you were simply referred to Holmyard.)

He joined in, with vigour, anything that took his fancy, and among his fancies was the Steyning cricket team. A mid-week team played relatively light-heartedly. The really serious cricket was played on Saturday. Shocker captained the mid-week Eleven and drafted in senior boarders if places needed to be filled. Thus it was that I saw Flab hoist a huge six over the pavilion and onto the roof of the Police Station. Both the ball and a slate broken by it, descended into the yard and onto a new and shining black police car which was being admired by the Sergeant and P.C. They appeared on the boundary holding the evidence and, from there, relieved themselves of a number of pent-up frustrations.

On another occasion I was about six feet away from the action, fielding at silly mid-on, with Flab bowling what he claimed to be leg-breaks, when he let the ball slip. It went about twenty feet into the air. The batsman prepared himself eagerly and everyone else took cover. The ball came down precisely on top of the wicket, squirting the bails off. The batsman had taken two inaccurate swipes at it as it came down and had to be forcibly restrained from turning his bat on Flab, who was by this time rolling on the ground, helpless with laughter.

Another 'savage' cricketer on the staff was Ike Williams. He had been a Commando in the war, helping partisans in Greece, where a bullet had blown his right shoulder-blade to pieces. In spite of this, he bowled at extreme pace and with great hostility. He blamed his shoulder - or lack of it - for the fact that neither he nor anyone else knew whether the next ball was going to be a beamer or a bouncer, whether it would scatter the stumps to the wide or merely decapitate second slip. He played his cricket in Storrington, but we experienced him first-hand in staff matches.

Ike was one of my mentors in the VI Form, where he taught zoology. We had the advantage of taking 'S' Level zoology as well as 'A' Level, and, while the 'A' Level papers could be passed simply by regurgitating things learnt by heart, the 'S' Level paper expected you to develop the thinking and show that you could marshall information to give support to your argument. The standard theory and practical elements were therefore interspersed in class with lively discussions during which he would put forward notions - not all to do with zoology - which he invited us to challenge. For those staying on after 'A' Levels, to take university entrance exams, this element of work grew. Evolutionary theory was, of course, on this menu. This led into theology. Ike was a practising Roman Catholic and, for the sake of argument, as well as from conviction, advanced dogma with a zeal in which a Jesuit would have taken pride. We donned the mantle of Huxley, and the battle between church and scientific realism was re-enacted. Arthur Lee, who declared he was an atheist, aided and abetted by introducing us to outlandish and outrageous notions with which we could tempt Ike into battle again.

It was done deliberately to get us to stretch our minds; to think and to challenge; never to take other people's ideas on trust; and to realise that as time goes by so ideas and understanding shift to give new patterns. It was a precious realisation given to me by the school in the late 1950s, that just because something is there in black and white in a text-book, it is not necessarily true. If you felt that the information on which a widely held concept was based was false - and could show it to be so - or that the information could be re-arranged to give a more pleasing pattern, then you should have the courage to say so. History is a potent weapon and a constant warning in science. How many of the established 'truths' of a thousand, a hundred, or even ten years ago do we smile at now? Rest assured, we will be smiled at ourselves a hundred years hence.

While that was one product of discussions with Ike, there was another lesson he encouraged us to draw from them. It was this: that the human mind (soul) needs a fixed point as an anchor; a bed-rock to give support. His was his Catholic faith. For us it might be something other, but without a point of reference there was the risk of unsettling and unsatisfying drift. Archimedes said: "Give me but one firm spot on which to stand, and I will move the earth". Ike wanted us to find our own firm spot, the *pou sto* from which we might indeed move the earth.

My other main mentor in my final years at Steyning was Joe Luker who, in teaching the VI Form, was able to concentrate on his main interest, botany. The junior classes he took for biology and, indeed, for chemistry, in which he kept one chapter ahead of the class! While in the VI Form it was xylem and phloem, the parts of a flower, using a flora, and slicing thin sections from stems with cut-throat razors, in the lower school tadpoles and metamorphosis were also involved.

One year we managed to introduce a couple of great diving beetle larvae into the second year's tadpole tank, which sat on a corner of the teacher's raised lab bench. These larvae are voracious predators and wasted no time decimating - or worse - the wriggling throng. It took Joe a while to register the horrified fascination induced in the second year class. When he came to see us, in the certain knowledge that we were responsible, he remarked:

"Coo blimey! I thought I'd really interested them, until I found those blinking beetle grubs. I had to switch from metamorphosis to food chains thanks to you lot!"

To get the authentic flavour of Joe's trademark "Coo blimey!", the "Coo" is said in a semi-falsetto and pronounced "Kew", and "blimey" is said in a normal register and pronounced "bloimee". Slightly different emphasis allowed it to be used as an expression of surprise, horror, regret, or simply as a prefatory remark.

Joe was a great believer in the benefit of practical experience. Book-learning, supplemented with his own duplicated notes issued to us to update or clarify the text-books, gave way quite regularly to walks onto the Downs, or along the dykes in the Adur flood-plain to study plants in the wild and to collect specimens for identification, micro-preparation and so on. The announcement: "Roight everybody! Tomorrow will be a botney walk!" was always a welcome one.

A Botany walk on the Adur flood-plain

Suitably equipped with notebooks, floras, vasculums, quadrats, magnifying glasses and the other impedementia deemed necessary, off we would trail. On arrival at the chosen spots we would set about our allotted tasks and identify the different plants, usually to a running commentary from Joe, interspersed with queries from us:

"Please, sir! I can't find this one in the flora. Can you show me?"

"Let's see. What have you got? Coo blimey! Squinancy-wort!"

Joe was also resident master in Coombe Court and sponsor of the Natural History Society, which I helped resurrect and which used an upper room on the 'dangerous' side of the building. More of this later!

There were, of course, other masters - Mr Gooderson who with his wife and daughters lived in Wykeham Cottage; Keith Sorrell; Mr Parkinson who was often 'ragged' by the boys and Mr Hollis who assumed that mantle when he left; Mr Harvey the geography master in 1952, who then left to go to the West Indies and was replaced by Mr Walters, who was in turn replaced by Mr Mabey who gave way to Mr Sauvain; John Alabone, the art master and Mr Chapman, who filled in for him for a year; Mr Shrewsbury, a retired industrial chemist who tried, with small success, to teach chemistry and who left in less than a year; Mr Prethero whose gentle sarcasm was greatly enjoyed; Mr Purver who inherited Coombe Court when Joe got married - to one of Mr Gooderson's daughters. While many will have bulked large in the lives of my contemporaries, I have sketched the ones who impinged most on me. Some of the others we will meet later.

The major omission so far is the Headmaster, John Scragg. He is a key figure, ever-present and all-pervasive. His study was the nerve-centre of the school, from which little went un-noticed. When Johnny said 'Come' you came; when he said 'Go' you went. With me it was more usually: "Pull your socks up, boy!" (literally, most of the time), and socks were pulled up immediately. Although his word was very much our command, I do not think he was feared by anyone in the way, perhaps, we feared Jonah. Perhaps we realised, instinctively, that behind the headmaster's mask he wore was a kind and humourous person who really did care about us. Since it is very much his school I am describing, I will do that first and then come back to Johnny to see whether in doing so it makes any sense of everything.

Before leaving the staff for the fabric of the school, some other important people need introduction.

Matron and Nurse were both resident in Main School. For all the time I was there, except for my first year, Miss Astrid Andersson was Matron. She was tall, fair and Swedish, but had been, I believe, a RAF nurse during the war and spoke with only a mild accent. She was a nice person, but stood no nonsense and few people pulled the wool over Matron's eyes. She didn't like fuss, and it was in character that, in 1964, when she was dying of cancer, she kept this from the boys who were simply told next term what had happened. She is buried in the churchyard. The Nurse's post was filled by Alison Gamble for most of my VI Form school-days. She was young and pretty and half the boarders were in love with her! The queue of senior boys was noticeably longer for surgery when Nurse was on duty than when Matron was.

Eventually, Matron stepped in. She asked to see me and Graham (Pop) Russell, the two most senior prefects in Holland House. Just before Nurse was due to arrive, we were to block the exits to make sure no-one left and then, instead of beautiful, blushing Ali Gamble there entered nasty old Matron wearing her best weathered-leather-boot face. No pleas were accepted of: "But Barker, I was only talking to Knowlden. I wasn't going to surgery." Matron did a roaring trade in nasty-tasting medicine and laxatives, and threats of spells in sick-bay on starvation diet were uttered.

Thereafter, an irregular pattern was introduced which meant that no-one was ever quite sure who would be taking surgery. Only the extremely brave or extremely fool-hardy were prepared to take the risk.

Of course, when Ali Gamble left, the collection for her present was huge. She received it after breakfast in the dining hall, with the presentation being made by one of her most ardent admirers, who was elected to this office by common consent. Everyone then sang:

"Goodbye Ali, goodbye!
Goodbye Ali, goodbye!
We will see you again,
But we don't know when.
Goodbye Ali, goodbye!"

and applauded most heartily. The result was entirely predictable - except to us - and Matron had to put an arm round her and escort her out to recover. It really didn't occur to us that an expression of gratitude, admiration and affection of this kind, and under these circumstances, could have the impact of a sledge-hammer on the recipient.

If Matron and Nurse were essential for our well-being, the school caretakers were essential for the well-being of the fabric of the school. It was Mr Nash and Mr Savage who later were joined by Mr Newman, who stoked the boilers; did minor running repairs to buildings and furniture; rang the bells which regulated our lives; swept corridors and classrooms; and tended the vegetable gardens at Coombe Court and, until the new dining hall was built on it, Wykeham House and cut the lawns - including the Sacred Turf of the Headmaster's lawn, on which no unauthorised foot dare tread. I swear that lawn had sensors in it, rigged to alarm bells in Johnny's study and in Holland Cottage. If you put one foot on it, the Headmaster suddenly materialised at your side, no matter what time of day or night.

In those days, the Headmaster's wife was expected to be active in running the school. However, Johnny wanted this association to be clearly defined, low profile so far as the boys were concerned, and separated from the work of other staff. Mrs Scragg therefore had responsibility for the domestic staff, including their recruitment.

As boarders, we were only familiar with the tip of the iceberg. We knew the maids who helped serve in the dining hall and who cleaned the Main School dormitories, Dormer, Wykeham and Coombe Court and we knew the Caterer - always, but inaccurately, called by us the cook.

When I arrived, the caterer was the diminutive, but fierce, Miss Agate - we saw her slay with her walking stick a goose which attacked her as she crossed a field on her way to school one morning! She then gave way to the large and fiery Mrs Barnes. Under the caterer were two cooks. There were then not just the four or five maids who cleaned the dormitories, helped with the washing up, cut the slogs and helped in the dining hall, but also a veritable army of part-time helpers behind the scenes. Preparing food three times a day for a hundred boarders is a lot of work, and the high-speed washing up needed to have back-to-back servings of lunch needs many hands!

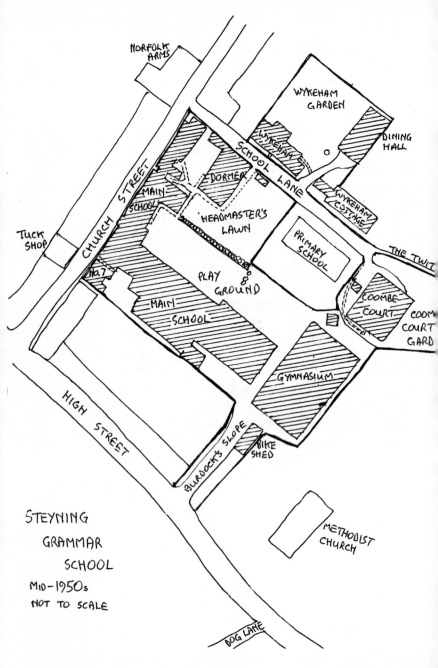

NORFOLK ARMS

WYKEHAM GARDEN

DINING HALL

SCHOOL LANE

WYKEHAM

WYKEHAM COTTAGE

CHURCH STREET

MAIN SCHOOL

DORMER

HEADMASTER'S LAWN

TUCK SHOP

No. 7

PLAY GROUND

PRIMARY SCHOOL

THE TWIT

MAIN SCHOOL

COOMBE COURT

COOM COURT GARD

GYMNASIUM

HIGH STREET

BURDOCK'S SLOPE

BIKE SHED

STEYNING
GRAMMAR
SCHOOL
MID-1950s
NOT TO SCALE

METHODIST CHURCH

DOG LANE

40

Chapter 2

Bewildered in the maze of schools

As the school expanded from the Brotherhood Hall nucleus between the 1920s and the 1950s, it spread along Church Street from Holland Cottage to No 7, and down The Twitten to take in Dormer, Wykeham House, Wykeham Cottage and Coombe Court. Buildings were pushed out into the spaces behind Brotherhood Hall to give the classrooms, laboratories and the gymnasium. In the centre of this complex were the Headmaster's lawn, separated by an evergreen hedge, iron railings and wire chain-link fence from the playground and, at a lower level, over a wall and fence at the lower end of the playground, fronting The Twitten and opposite Wykeham Cottage, was Steyning's Church of England Primary School. (I know it is inaccurate to call School Lane 'The Twitten', since The Twitten proper starts by Coombe Court and runs to Jarvis Lane, but we always referred to both as The Twitten and I will continue to do so!)

Construction in 1950/51 of the physics lab had divided the playground into two. The main area, with a small group of large trees, lay between the labs and the Headmaster's lawn. A gap, wide enough to take a fire-engine, ran between the gym and the end of the physics lab, into a small playground, which flanked the main toilets and the physics lab. From this, Burdock's Slope ran down to double gates into the High Street. At the top of Burdock's Slope and at the end of the gym were the school bike sheds, used by day boys.

When I arrived at the school, there were no classrooms above the physics laboratory and the gym was a separate building. To get to either meant going across the playground - demanding a quick dash if it was raining.

For the boarders in Wykeham and in Coombe Court, extra play-space was there in the form of the gardens. The lawns were available to us, but not the vegetable gardens - unless the edict had gone out that we were to weed them, or gather specified produce. Needless to say,

41

carefully planned raids were made, with look-outs meticulously posted, to grab carrots, peas or broad beans. On Wykeham lawn was a huge mulberry tree, the biggest in Sussex. Its fruit began to ripen by the end of the summer term, and delicious it was - and frightful were the comments of Matron about boys who got clothes stained by the berries! Dormer had no boys' garden since that was partly the Headmaster's lawn and partly his rose beds. However, alongside The Twitten was an air-raid shelter, a relic of the war and, until it was demolished in the mid-1950s, it was used as a place in which we could make model aeroplanes and test the little petrol engines which powered them. With the combination of glue, dope and fuel in a confined space it is amazing we never blew the place up or anaesthetised ourselves. Conscious solvent abuse was unheard of then, but many were addicted to dope!

The main entrance to the school was from Church Street, under the Brotherhood Hall tower. Double wrought-iron gates, closed only in the holidays, gave onto a heavy wooden door, locked and bolted just before boarders' tea and unlocked again after breakfast. A short, steep flight of stairs led up to the Big School landing. On the left as you went in was a door which took you down a few steps into the dining hall - later converted into the library. The kitchens, into which we were not admitted, lay to the right as you went into the dining hall, as did a large, gas-fired hot-plate on which tea urns and trays of food were placed. On the wall at that lower end of the hall was a wooden cupboard in which boarders kept their personal and carefully labelled jars of jam, boxes of cheese spread and jars of marmite, meat paste, or honey - if they had any. Reserve supplies were kept in your tuck-boxes. You were allowed only one jar in the cupboard at a time and Matron periodically inspected the contents, and firmly jettisoned what she considered to be *salmonella* surprises, usually to the vocal regret of the owners.

To the right of Big School landing was Big School with its massive beams and diamond-paned, leaded windows. At the far end was the piano to the right, a large cupboard to the left and, in the centre, a low wooden dais, raised perhaps nine inches above the floor and on which a heavy oak table stood with a teacher's chair behind it. Over this was an electric light with a metal shade which made a splendidly resonant target for pellets - if you had the courage! Other, less risky targets were the shades of lights hanging in the body of the room. It was also possible to persuade cockchafers, captured in the playground, to fly during prep to bang into it and fall onto the duty master or prefect sat at the table. On the wall behind the dais were the blackboards. Double desks, with wooden chairs, occupied the floor and in these the first year and second year boarders kept their books. At the back of Big School was the House Prefects' room, up a few wooden steps and, in a small central alcove, a First World War brass memorial tablet and the boarders' post box. Behind the door was the Holland House noticeboard.

Just beyond Big School and also to the right, you went up a step into the tile-floored Chancton Lobby. I imagine that in earlier times this had been the school washroom but now was reduced to a row of wash-basins under windows looking out across the roof of the Main School boiler house and into the courtyard leading to No 7. The centre of Chancton Lobby, and the other walls, were occupied by the tall wooden lockers in which the day boys of Chancton House kept their books, coats and games kits.

To the left from Big School landing, you went through a door which gave onto a steep flight of wooden stairs which curved precipitously up into the washroom used by all the boarders living in Main School - the residents of Long Dorm, Upper Dorm and Junior Dorm, plus the Holland House Captain. We were adept at going up and down these stairs at great speed and, although sometimes your descent was a little more rapid than you had planned and conducted using parts of your anatomy not employed in the normal run of events, or your ascent, and dignity, marred as you missed your footing, I cannot recall any serious injuries.

To get into Long Dorm itself, you went through a second door. Immediately to the left on entry was the dormitory captain's cubicle. He had the privilege of being able to keep his light on long after lights-out for the first year boys. Those in the two beds nearest the cubicle had enough light to read by - just - but it was risky to try this, especially if Jonah was on the prowl. At the far end, to the right of a door leading into Matron's Corridor, was a large communal wardrobe in which were kept Sunday suits. Outdoor coats were kept on pegs in Matron's Corridor. Something in the order of twenty beds were spaced along the walls, each with its wooden bed-side locker and the space between beds was just slightly more than the width of the locker. On the right, and just over a bed's length from the door in from Big School landing, was a door, at the top of a couple of steps, into the school Surgery.

If you went out of Long Dorm at the far end and into Matron's Corridor you turned right and followed it along to the head of Matron's stairs. These led down into the staff hall and only staff and prefects could use them. Just before the stairs was Matron's lavatory (used also by those incarcerated in sick-bay) and at the head of the stairs, on the right, was Matron's bathroom. This too was used by boys in sick-bay and it was a sure sign that you were about to be let out when you were commanded to go to it to have a bath. On one or two occasions wires got crossed, and boys found themselves in competition with Nurse for rights of occupancy. Proceeding further along the corridor, Matron's sitting-room was to the right, with a window from it onto the playground. Straight ahead was a door into what in 1951/52 was an overspill dormitory for Long Dorm and known as Junior Dorm. By 1953 it was one of two sick-bay rooms. The second lay along a corridor leading to the left and was immediately over the Headmaster's study. Each sick-bay held about half-a-dozen beds and these normally gave more than enough space. Only in the Asian 'flu outbreak in the mid-1950s did the accommodation prove inadequate, and then the whole of Long Dorm and, I believe, Dormer, were pressed into service.

Stairs by second sick-bay led up to private rooms occupied by Matron, Nurse and the maids. No male foot was allowed to desecrate these stairs. It was possible, but risky, to reach the windows to the maids' rooms by climbing over the roof, as Pop Russell and I discovered, but the risks of detection by Matron or of death by over-

44

precipitate descent outweighed the benefits of whispered conversation, which was all that was possible. Although Margaret and Mary were impressed by our enterprise, they too made it plain that the risks to their livelihoods were ones they were not prepared to run.

Back on Big School landing, there was the school timetable on the left side, by the door through to Long Dorm. Half way across the landing was a structure known as The Beam on which was the school clock, facing away from Church Street and towards the playground. The playground and Lower Corridor were reached down a flight of shallow and worn stone steps. The older boys could get up or down this flight in three or four strides. Just beyond The Beam, and at the head of these stairs, was an alcove in which the laundry baskets were stored. The stairs down were to the left side of the landing. To the right side, were stairs up to Upper Corridor.

The school clock was a recognised meeting spot for boarders planning to do things together. Two people planning to go on a cross-country run almost always sealed the arrangements with the words: "I'll see you under the clock at four". First-years were commanded to meet 'under the clock' at specified times before setting off to be guided to some hitherto unvisited place or as yet unencountered experience. Joint expeditions to spend our meagre pocket-money in Steyning's emporia frequently were launched from 'under the clock'.

Meeting under the clock....

Going into Upper Corridor, there were, on the left at the top of the stairs, a set of small lockers for VI Formers' books. The corridor went half the width of the building to the right before turning left at right angles to run the length of the building. The school noticeboard was on the right-hand wall of the shorter first section. Straight ahead, as the corridor swung left, was the stationery cupboard. Here, at specified times, a duty master issued new stationery on request - well almost on request! You had to bring with you the evidence that you needed a new exercise book, pencil or whatever. An exercise book had to be finished completely before a new one was issued and the duty master cut a corner off the front cover of the old one to prevent you, or anyone else, from presenting it again. A pencil had to be down to its last inch and you swapped the stub for a new one. The exercise books had the school badge printed on them in black and were coloured differently for each subject - red = history; grey = maths; green = English; blue = French and so on. These all had lined pages. The vital Rough Book had a less substantial orange/brown cover without a school badge, and plain pages. In this were done all rough notes, trial workings for maths problems, sketches taken from blackboard notes for working up neatly later, and into your Rough Book you copied assignments for prep. The Rough Book got special scrutiny to make sure it had no crevice of space into which more might be crammed and that it had not been used for illicit purposes, such as games of naughts and crosses or battleships. Paper for such activities was taken from the middle, if you were wise, but woe-betide you if the proffered exercise book seemed suspiciously thin.

Turning into the main length of the corridor, past the stationery cupboard and on the right was the school prefects' room. Until 1952 it had been the staff room, but they moved then into what had been a classroom and the adjoining school prefects' room, thus bringing the staff room next to the Headmaster's study. The next room down the corridor on the right was Room 7, which I associate primarily with Arthur Lee's history classes. It had a metal pipe in the back left-hand corner of the room which made a sonorous and easy target for Arthur's blackboard duster if he felt someone was day-dreaming.

On the left of the corridor were three classrooms. The first, Room 4, I remember being used for English and French and in this room the senior boarders, basically Remove 1 and Remove, did their prep in the evening supervised by a prefect. The junior boarders used Big School for this purpose. VI Formers were unsupervised and used various common-rooms, the library or, in a few cases, personal desks in dormitories.

The second, Room 5, was the special preserve of the senior maths master - Jonah for my first couple of years and then Glubbie. Revisiting the school in 2000, I was interested to see that the original woodwork is still there. The cupboards, blackboard and shelves in the front are as they were, and, standing close to them, I almost felt again the chalk in my trembling hand, a hand cuffing my head and a voice saying: "Think, boy! Think!" These small landmarks mean a lot to someone returning to the place after nearly fifty years, as I was doing.

At the bottom of the corridor, a door to the left led into the art room, Room 6. The room extended for its full length beyond the door, but the corridor ended at the art room portal until the late 1950s when two classrooms were built above the physics lab and the corridor extended to serve them. A door to the right gave onto an outside, metal staircase which led along the edge of the Bog roof and down into the small playground at the top of Burdock's Slope. This was the fire escape, but was used every day by everyone as part of the general network connecting the various parts of the school. From the Bog flat roof a vertical metal ladder led onto the flat roof over Room 7 and the school prefects' room, and the flat roof continued round the pitched roofs of Rooms 4 and 5 to the windows into Upper Dorm. This route was the fire escape from Upper Dorm and was only used, officially, during fire drill or if there were to be a fire. Needless to say, it was in pretty regular use, unofficially, by VI Formers and I well remember sitting up there with friends, talking and watching the sunset while parties of screaming swifts hurtled around the buildings of the town, coming almost close enough to touch.

The layout of Lower Corridor was basically similar to that of Upper Corridor. Here, however, was the main block of day boys'

Parties of screaming swifts……

lockers and a battery of coat-hooks for day boys too. At the angle of the corridor was a door to the right which led into a small courtyard behind the kitchens and in which was the Main School boiler house. A 'tradesmans' entrance led into this courtyard from Church Street and deliveries to the kitchens were made through it. Boys were not allowed to use it. From the courtyard was a route round to No 7. This was where the shoe-cleaning kit was kept for the inhabitants of Long Dorm, Junior Dorm and Upper Dorm. Here too, when I first arrived, was a bathroom and changing room and in 1951/52 there was a master's flat on the upper level in which Spud Crannigan lurked.

Alongside the classroom block and at the back of No 7 was what we called No 7 Garden. It was basically uncultivated, but gave a source of specimens for biology lessons. A few years before I arrived, boys had constructed a small, concrete-lined pond. This was resuscitated periodically and mutually incompatible selections of pond-life added. This was also a source of specimens which Ike Williams and Joe Luker used to better our education.

Back in the Lower Corridor, a boot locker room was the equivalent of the stationery cupboard in Upper Corridor. Next on the right was the chemistry prep room and chemical store. Beyond that was Room 3 which, by the time I left, had become the biology lab. It had a raised demonstration bench at the front, below the blackboards. Standard desks gave way eventually to solid tables and lab stools, and it was here that we cut up earthworms, dog-fish, frogs and rats in the VI Form and went to lunch thereafter smelling so highly of formalin that the rest put a *cordon sanitaire* around us.

To the left of the corridor and occupying the space under Rooms 4 and 5 was the chemistry lab and beyond it and below the art room was the woodwork room with its fixed wooden benches, much scarred by misdirected tools and each with two vices and sets of basic tools. You worked two to a bench, but on opposite sides of it. At the bottom end of the woodwork room was a store in which your work in progress was kept. Jamie would place the best pieces of work near the window onto the playground so that people could admire them. It worked. There was always a good deal of interest in that ever-changing display.

At the bottom of the corridor, a double door led into the small playground, and the entry to the Bog was on the right as you went out. Another entry to the Bog was from the small playground itself. The physics lab was on the left and had two doors in from the small playground. Behind the demonstration desk and blackboards was the physics prep room. For a short while we used this as a VI Form biology lab. This was inconvenient all round, since to get into or out of it you had to disturb the lesson being given in the physics lab.

Beyond the physics lab was the gym. The gym doubled as the Assembly Hall for the school and had a stage on which school plays were presented and on which the staff sat at morning Assembly. The folding chairs used for plays and Speech Day were stored under the stage, and a hot and dusty job it was to be sent in to get these chairs out or to replace them. At the back of the stage were two doors into the changing room and showers. A short flight of concrete steps gave access to the changing room from the small playground and this was the prescribed route in if you were doing gym. Two sets of double doors led from the main playground into the body of the gym and these were used by the boys at morning assembly.

Because certain activities could take place only in specially equipped places, every forty-five minutes saw a general *mêlée* along the communications network I have outlined. Add to that the classrooms and occasionally-used rooms in the other buildings, and there was a good deal of rapid movement when the bell went.

Imagine too, after the day boys had gone home, how the boarders could make use of the system. A chase starting round Coombe Court might rocket up The Twitten - slowed only if: "*Walk*, boy!" came from Wykeham Cottage - round Dormer, with a rapid application of brakes past the speed-traps of Johnny's study and the staff room, and then, down the playground, round the trees, back to the stairs, up to the clock and into Upper Corridor, down the fire escape, a couple of turns using the two ways into the Bog, along Lower Corridor - and so on. The main hazards were progressively made safer - for example, in 1952, glass with wire mesh embedded substituted for plain glass in the doors into Lower Corridor after Minnie Mansell put his hand through a window when his quarry swung the door back in his face during a high speed chase and sliced through tendons and blood-vessels in spectacular fashion.

At the top end of the main playground was at first one and, later, after the new dining hall had been built and the kitchens moved, two significant rooms. Both were reached from a pathway alongside the staff room which was separated by iron railings from the playground. Room 13 was the place where, when I first arrived, the first year boarders kept their books in desks. We used it as an alternative Common Room too. It had a door with a large window in it at the back. This was kept locked, but it led into the hallway at the staff entrance and many were the times when the blood was chilled by an angry tapping on the window and the disinheriting countenance of Johnny or Jonah glaring in at you. Room 13 was, later, used just for VI Form classes.

The other room was a half-basement in the old kitchen from which a window opened into the playground area. Here in breaks selected boys ran a school tuck shop.

If, from the playground, you walked towards Dormer and, just past the Headmaster's study turned left, the path led to Holland Cottage in which the Scragg family lived, but the path also had a left fork which led to a door into the staff entrance hall. Straight ahead at this door was Lower Library, the main reference library for the school. This was available at all times, although juniors had to ask permission first. Lower Library had no ceiling and you looked up into Upper Library, its shelves containing assorted, and officially approved, novels. I recall that the works of G.A. Henty, Rider Haggard, John Buchan, Dickens and Conan Doyle featured amongst others. Access (official that is) was a narrow staircase which went up to the left along an equally narrow corridor leading to the school Secretary's and Bursar's office. This staircase led also to a staff flat occupied in my first year by Jonah and later by Slopey Joe Baker. The Upper Library was opened to boarders by the Holland House Librarian - usually a House Prefect appointed by the Housemaster - at lunch hour on Wednesdays and Saturdays. Solemn and bureaucratic were the procedures undertaken to record returns and withdrawals, and severe and rigorously imposed were the fines. The Librarian occupied a cubby-hole in one corner and into this had been built, years before by the ornithologist and teacher Stanley Bayliss-Smith, a nest box for swifts with an observation panel in it. Unofficial access by senior boarders wanting a bit of light - well lightish - reading was to swing up from the Lower Library, using a beam which crossed the well, and to hop over the railings which prevented juniors being dislodged from the gallery in the scrum for the best books.

In the early 1950s, the Secretary's and Bursar's office was further along the narrow corridor and left through a tiny room in which the first year boarders kept their tuck-boxes. The Junior Common Room was to the right and here we had a table and some chairs and were provided with the *Daily Mail*. Quite early in my school career the tuck-box room and Junior Common Room were converted into more school offices.

I have taken a bit of trouble to describe the maze of Main School. It was into this that about twenty rather nervous small boys were dropped one traumatic evening in September 1951. It took a while to chart our way, and frantic were the arguments between us when we lost our bearings between the assorted activities of the day. I will deal more swiftly with the other buildings. Their shells and basic internal structures remain more or less the same now as they were then. The uses to which different bits are put now do differ, sometimes radically, from those with which we were familiar and I will try to give a flavour of these. I make an exception of Coombe Court, which is no more. I was senior prefect in Coombe Court in 1957/58 and 1958/59 and a dormitory captain for a year in 1955/56 and knew it intimately. It was uncomfortable, inconvenient, dangerous, far removed from the sanitised luxury, as we would have seen it, of modern accommodation for boarders, but it was also huge fun, totally unconventional even by our standards, and it generated an *ésprit de corps* all of its own. I would not have missed it for anything!

After my first year we were all moved out of Long Dorm to make way for the next intake. We were scattered like hay-seeds, and in the second year I was successively in Dormer, Wykeham and Coombe Court, and we mixed in, sometimes uncomfortably, with boys a year or so older. Let us start, as I did, with Dormer. From the path outside the Headmaster's study, a ramp led down to the way in. Of course, when it rained, water ran off the higher ground and down the ramp. From time to time the drain at the bottom got blocked, and, I confess, this process sometimes was given our help, and a considerable pool developed. Indeed on one occasion it invaded the building. As soon as the cry went up: "Please, sir! Dormer Bank's flooded again!", boys were sent round to the front door in The Twitten - under normal circumstances boys were not allowed to use it - to go and put on Wellingtons. Some were then launched into the flood to try to remove the blockage. At the same time, a wise master would have sent out a search party for one of the caretakers, because our efforts frequently made a bad situation worse. By this time the rumpus would have brought Johnny out, under an umbrella, from study or house and with him standing grimly at the top of the slope it was usual to find a degree of efficiency, hitherto missing, being brought to bear.

Dormer Bank is flooded again!

Apart from the music room on the right of the door, which I have already mentioned, there were two rooms on the right as you moved along the hall towards the front door and stairs. The first, which had French windows out onto the path running down past the air-raid shelter to The Twitten, was first a Common Room and then a dormitory. The second was a Common Room throughout. I think that the newspaper here was the long gone *Daily Herald*. To the left of the hall was a toilet (a second toilet was over it on the first floor) and then the changing room with all our games kit and Wellingtons. The changing room held the boiler. The coke, with which it was fed, was kept outside in a small courtyard reached by going through the bathroom and showers.

Upstairs were two floors of dormitories - two on each - and the resident master, Drip Walters in my time there, had his living room/study on the first floor, above the changing room and his bedroom on the second floor, above his study. Each dormitory held six or seven boys and in each there was an older boy or a prefect as dormitory captain. These made free use of the slipper to punish crimes such as talking after lights-out.

On the first floor and above the ground floor music room, was a small bathroom. There were no wash-basins. Each bedside locker had on top of it an enamelled metal bowl and in that an enamelled metal jug. Water was collected from the bathrooms in the jug and taken back to the dormitory. Having washed your face, hands and torso while standing up by your locker, the basin was put on the floor and you sat on the edge of your bed and washed your feet. It was as I completed this one evening that I was attacked by Bill Jacobs, my neighbour, who suspected, correctly, that I had put something down his bed. After a brief wrestling match on my bed, Bill rolled off and onto the edge of my basin. This flipped up and finished upside-down across his knees as he sat on the floor. Many and loud were the complaints from the dormitory beneath as water seeped through the ceiling and onto beds and their occupants.

Washing in Dormer

Although there were regular minor spillages, catastrophic spillage of this size was generally on the stairs. The reason was that the top floor had no bathroom and its occupants had to trudge down to the first floor to get water. There was a good deal of scope for boys to collide or to miss their footing and the bucket, mop and floor cloth from the maid's cupboard were in frequent use. While we all treated this light-heartedly, lightning struck from time to time. Once, a bowl of water, dropped at the top of the stairs, timed things so as to irrigate Jonah as he began the ascent on his rounds as duty master. There was an immediate kangaroo court, the case for the prosecution being that the boy should have had the water in a jug and not in a bowl. Herein lay the dilemma facing those on the top floor. Once you had finished washing, you could try pouring the water back into the jug from the basin. This was not easy and if you misjudged things you spilled water. On the other hand, you could risk carrying the bowl of water along the corridor, down the stairs and along the first floor corridor to the bathroom. Again, not easy without risking spillage or, as in this case, half-drowning your Housemaster in water previously used for washing your feet.

While I was in one of the top floor dormitories, I was once relieved of this choice when my dormitory captain tipped my bowl out of the window, having spied a couple of his friends passing beneath. Although in keeping with mediaeval tradition, such practices were discouraged, and dreadful was your fate should the presence of Johnny on his lawn have gone unnoticed when you tried it.

Conditions were better in Wykeham. Generally speaking, this building was reserved for older boys - Remove 1, Remove and the VI Form - but in my second year, as well as me, a number of Remove 2 boys were there. The resident master, Digger Gardener, had a flat at the top of the building. There were proper washrooms on the first and ground floors and, in the early 1950s, the whole building had been re-decorated and refurbished. Only staff and VI Formers used the front door in from The Twitten. Everyone else went in past the coke shed and into the changing rooms at the Wykeham Cottage end of the building. A corridor led from this, past a cloak-room, washroom, bathroom and toilet, and then gave onto a junction with a dormitory straight ahead, a way out into the garden on the right, and up a couple of wooden steps into the first of three Common Rooms. At one point in my career, I believe in 1954/55, I was dormitory captain in the ground floor dormitory, Garden Dorm. Since I went to bed myself after lights-out, my bed was straight ahead as you went in through the door so I could get a little light to undress in without disturbing the others. In the wall towards and beyond the foot of the bed was an alcove with a low, wide ledge. On this I kept a vivarium housing a couple of slow-worms which I fed on small white slugs found in the garden - feeding time usually drew an audience! I also had a microscope, which someone had given to my father, and two huge glass jars used as aquaria for pond-life. I spent a lot of time peering at pond animals and microscopic organisms sucked up from these aquaria. At around this time, much to Johnny's frequently expressed misgivings, misgivings in no way allayed, may I say, when he saw the gentleman concerned perform on TV, Elvis Presley was in vogue. Someone had a couple of his records and these were played incessantly on the Wykeham gramophone. To this day I smell pondwater whenever I hear *Hound Dog* or *Singing the Blues*!

The first of the three Common Rooms was the General Common Room and into it the front door opened. It was here that Mr Presley's musical achievements were played and admired and here, on a table, that the morning paper was placed, I think by now we had graduated to the *Daily Telegraph*. From this open room you went through, to the right as you came in through the front door, into a quiet room. This was for reading, quiet conversation and other relaxing quiet pursuits. Elvis was definitely banned from crossing the threshold. Passing through the quiet room, you went through a door and down a couple of steps into the TV room. You could also get into the TV room from outside through a door leading from the drive into Wykeham Cottage, but this door was normally locked.

The TV room came about when an Old Boy, Tom Breach, died. He lived in Steyning at the junction of Station Road with Cripps Lane. From time to time, until his last illness, junior boarders were invited in groups of half-a-dozen to have afternoon tea with him and to watch the television. What excitement! Many of us had never seen a television before and the large and heavy machine, with its magnifying lens over the screen in its polished walnut cabinet with the doors you opened out when you were watching it, was clearly at the cutting edge of modern technology. I cannot remember what I watched on the couple of occasions I was privileged to go to tea; it was wonder enough that there were pictures of any kind - even if 'snow storms' were frequent too.

When he died, the kind old man left the television to the school. That a special room be dedicated to it shows the respect it was afforded. Groups of specially selected and privileged boys were allowed to see carefully vetted programmes. Shakespeare's plays were among these, and you always hoped that the BBC would put on the one you were doing in English literature, because that guaranteed a seat. Every other Saturday evening, groups of boarders - those who had committed no detected crimes, those who had missed out on previous occasions, and those who could blackmail the duty prefect - were able to watch the visual banquet prepared for them by Auntie. Usually, Johnny would look in to reassure himself that we were not watching rubbish or anything likely to corrupt or inflame. If he got interested, the person in the middle of the front row was hoisted from his chair so he could sit and watch for a while. Two programmes I saw still stick in my mind. One was episodes of *Quatermass and the Pit*, which terrified me. The other was a magical production of *Under Milkwood* in which proper use was made of the possibilities opened up by television, with fade-in-fade-out and superimposed or multiple imagery used. I still see in my mind Captain Cat dreaming of his long-dead mess-mates; Polly Garter singing of Little Willie Wee and of Tom, Dick and Harry; the Reverend Eli Jenkins mourning the loss of his father to 'drink and agriculture' and his prayer for those living in the village 'under Milkwood'; and No-Good Boyo, with whom many of us empathised.

It was in the TV room too that I fell foul of authority when I found a stink-horn fungus and placed pieces on top of the picture-rail. As the nearest person to hand with biological qualifications, Joe Luker was brought in to cast light on the possible source of the stench. He, being a good field botanist, identified the smell correctly, but was unable to trace its source. As sponsor of the Natural History Society and as VI Form botany master, he had little trouble in fingering me as culprit. I was commanded, in no uncertain terms, to remove the fragments; to do so immediately; and to indulge in future in no foolish tricks which meant his being disturbed while he was enjoying a quiet snooze.

Wykeham garden was a privilege enjoyed by boys in Wykeham. The mulberry tree provided shade under its spreading and propped-up branches, as well as fruit in season, if we had an early summer. We set out croquet hoops on the lawn in the summer. Although the course was laid out more or less as the rules demanded and we played with mallets and regulation balls, that was the extent of our bow in the direction of convention. Youthful enthusiasm and the bumps in the lawn, produced a game which was to croquet about what Australian Rules Football is to Soccer. Great fun and highly dangerous. My abiding memory of Wykeham garden is lying on the grass revising for exams with the heady and distinctive scent of the *Philadelphus* flowing over us. I have grown *Philadelphus* in my own gardens ever since, but not, unfortunately, the tall variety with large single flowers still growing in Wykeham garden - that bush has been there for at least 60 years and probably longer. Just as *Singing the Blues* makes me smell pond water, so smelling *Philadelphus* makes me see Wykeham lawn on a warm summers day with small groups of people on the grass reading books. You did so at your peril, mind you, if a game of croquet was in progress!

Reading on Wykeham lawn

58

The only down side to the gardens of Wykeham and Coombe Court was, that once or twice a term, it was decreed that everyone would spend an hour doing gardening. This involved tearing out the most rampant weeds, breaking off stems of plants which had gone over, hoeing what purported to be gravel paths, edging lawns, picking up dead twigs fallen from the trees and replacing edging stones. However, you did not escape if you were in Dormer or Main School. A few 'trusties' were given the job of hoeing the gravel path. which ran the length of the Headmaster's lawn behind the hedge dividing it from the playground. There was an herbaceous border behind an apple tree at the end of the lawn which was also 'in play' for gardening, and I remember once, and under strict personal

There's a big beetle there, and it's bitten Hardy.

supervision, removing weeds from one of Johnny's rose-beds outside Dormer. The first year was sometimes unleashed on No 7 Garden, and it was this which led to periodic resuscitation of the pond there. If all else failed, there were the playgrounds and Burdock's Slope to tidy up. *Very* occasionally one or two boys were given jobs to do in the lean-to greenhouses on the end of Dormer beside the Headmaster's lawn and outside the staff room. It was the presence of these greenhouses immediately alongside the route to and from Coombe Court and Wykeham - and later the Dining Hall - and Main School, which explains the ferocity with which the 'no running' law along this stretch was enforced.

As an entomologist and collector of beetles, I quite welcomed gardening as license to find specimens. Naturally, others knew of my interest and, particularly when I had been made into that all-powerful being, Holland House Captain, juniors would bring in finds or call me to them if they looked too fierce:

"Please, Barker! Could you come round to No 7? There's a big beetle there, and it's bitten Hardy!"

This leaves us with Coombe Court! Originally two semi-detached houses for gentlemen - a very similar style building remains opposite Springwells in the High Street at its junction with Wykeham Close - this flint and brick-walled building housed a *mélange* of second and third-year boys. There was a half-basement and then three storeys, with the uppermost rooms under the roof and so with parts of their ceilings sloping. Each of the original dwellings was the mirror image of the other. Outside, on the Wykeham side of the building and on the boundary between the two, was an outside toilet under a single roof, but with a dividing wall down the centre. Each side held one flush toilet. The garden ran down to the bottom of the slope and at the bottom was a brick-built, tiled shed. Part of the Steyning Centre now occupies the lower bit of the garden where the shed stood.

The half of Coombe Court facing The Twitten was completely occupied by boarders. On the second floor, the wall dividing the two houses had been partly removed and the dormitories here were part in one half and part in the other. However the stairs going down on the far side were blocked with a wooden barrier to prevent their official use other than in emergency. The second floor dormitories had, therefore, access onto two landings and you could travel through these dormitories and across the landings in a circle. Raids made by one dormitory on the other could thus allow pincer movements. The layout meant, too, that no-one could predict in which direction authority would be moving - especially if it cheated and used the forbidden stairs. At the highest level, the two parts were connected only by emergency fire hatches. The far side rooms were not dormitories. One was the school trunk room; one was the Natural History Society room and a third was too unsafe to use and was in 1958 occupied only by a splendid specimen of dry rot fungus which we wanted to include in a Speech Day exhibit for parents to see. We were told that to do so would be 'courageous' and courage bowed to prudence!

There were no connections between the two parts at basement or first floor levels. The far side basement was the tuck-box room for Main School, Dormer and Wykeham. Two of the first floor rooms were used as classrooms and a small room was the Archaeology Society room.

Underlying this rather haphazard arrangement was the fact that the building was moving bodily down the slope. The walls on the far side were held up by a series of huge wooden support beams angled up from secure foundations to differing heights on the walls. Cracks continued to appear. The VI Form mathematicians who were taught by Glubbie in Room 11, once drew his attention to a fresh crack. He reassured them that it was perfectly OK and they only had to start worrying when they could see through it into the garden. Two weeks later they could! More support beams were installed.

On the 'safe' side, Joe Luker, the resident master, told us that he had been a bit puzzled when the Headmaster, briefing him on arrival, had asked whether he had a wireless set. Unsure what the significance was, he confirmed that he had indeed got a set. Do not, he was told, nail your aerial to the outside walls of your room. If you do, stones may fall off onto the drive. Very reassuring when your room is under the roof some twenty-five or thirty feet above the ground!

Entry on the far side to classrooms, tuck-box room and Archaeology Society room was through the front door. On the residential side, only staff and the dormitory captains were allowed to use the front door. Everyone else had to go down a flight of concrete steps by the outside toilet and into the half-basement. As you went in, you found yourself in the changing room in which were three showers with concrete basins, a bath and the boiler. An open doorway beyond the boiler led into a narrow room with pegs for your kit. There were also two spaces behind wooden slats; one was a boot room, the other was empty and kept locked. The coal-hole was at the end of the narrow room.

In 1955/56 the empty space was in constant, if clandestine, use by two of my contemporaries, Roger Barnwell and David Tas. They had acquired a derelict motorbike and by substituting their own padlock for the official one, gained a secure hidey-hole in which to take it to bits, clean everything, replace dud pieces, put it all together and paint it. They had their own light which they controlled from inside, and the whole population of boys acted as look-outs. The changing room gained a fine aroma of oil and paint to mix with boiler fumes and sweaty socks, but they remained undetected. On the last day of the summer term, after we had broken up officially, the bike, now painted a smart racing green, was hauled up the steps. Dai Tas claims that they got it started, but my last sight was of them running it up and down The Twitten trying to get it to fire.

The boiler was an impressive 'Queen Mary'. When there had been House games, Form games or cross-country runs, the boys would ensure plenty of hot water for showers by pulling out the damper before leaving. This was fine, so long as it had not been pulled out too far, or they forgot to push it in once they returned. Either meant that the water boiled. Steam then rose, noisily, up the pipes into the header tank in the first floor bathroom and the normally cold water in that became hot. The upstairs toilet was fed, not from the rising main, but from the header tank. Thus it was that Joe Luker once, using the toilet immediately after someone else, found himself flushing it with hot water: "Coo blimey! Look at that! Coombe Court has got all the mod cons!"

It was a perishing nuisance if the damper was left open in the evening. When I was building prefect I was sometimes woken up by the gurgling and banging which the steam made as it rose in the pipe. The technique was to get up, cursing; rush down to the changing room and push in the damper, assuming you could get near to the almost incandescent boiler; turn on all the hot taps you could find and stand well back. After ten explosive minutes you could turn the taps off and go back to bed with the whole of the stair-well as full of steam as a sauna.

Coombe Court has all the mod cons!

This was by no means the only trick of the Coombe Court plumbing. The header tank ball-cock was not entirely reliable and on a few occasions did not shut off properly. It was usually detected in time to nip flooding in the bud, or at least to confine it to the airing cupboard in the upstairs bathroom. Again, the technique was to turn on taps to draw it down, and you then made damned sure that the ball-cock was doing what ball-cocks should. One winter night in 1958 it saw its chance, and I was awoken by the sound of falling water. I was unable to move very fast having only the previous day been released from sick-bay after having had thirty stitches in a cut at the top of my leg. I located the cascade as water coming, in quantity, through the Common Room ceiling. Limping upstairs I turned on taps, blasphemed the ball-cock and, after bringing the source of the flood under control, limped back to find a bucket and mop. There seemed no point in waking up anyone else. The water had, by now, flowed merrily through the floorboards of the Common Room and was invading the changing room below. After some half an hour of mopping up and moving games kit from any pegs standing into danger, I was able to go back to bed, leaving an army of buckets and bowls to catch the worst of the drips. After casting an

63

eye at the Common Room ceiling, I did have the foresight to pin a note to the door prohibiting entry.

Next day saw the drying out process put in hand properly, and a large chunk of the ceiling spread out over table and floor to add to the gaiety of nations.

Returning to the basement, a door led from the changing room to the foot of the stairs up to the ground floor and opposite this door was another into the tuck-box room.

Going up the stairs you passed, through a door at the head, into the entry hall from the front door. Immediately to the left was the washroom with its long trestle tables on which the enamelled metal wash basins were spread - hence the ready supply to catch drips on the night of the flood. A deep stone sink in the far corner, with taps, was the source of water for the wash basins, and into it teeth were cleaned. Spillage in the washroom meant damp kit in the changing room, but it was rare that basins were dropped.

Also on the left was the Common Room. This was a large room with French windows leading out onto the gravelled drive in from The Twitten. Long wooden tables occupied the centre and a table-tennis table top could be put over them. On it many fierce matches were played. At the hall end of the room and against the outside wall was a huge flat-topped cupboard with sliding doors. Boys often sat on or lay along this monster, or stood at it to read the newspaper spread along it. In 1958 I spent hours leaning at it drawing fossils for my Trevelyan Scholarship thesis. The Coombe Court newspaper was the *Daily Express*. With so many boys wanting to look at the paper it was, of course, normal for it to be separated into its constituent pages and spread about on tables, the cupboard top and on the floor. Small clusters of boys gathered round each sheet jockeying for position to see the most popular bits, such as the back page with the sport and 'The Gambols' strip cartoon, or the inside page with the main cartoon - and great was our joy if it was a Giles cartoon! There were lockers in the Common Room on the wall between it and the washroom. In these the Coombe Court boarders kept their books.

On the opposite side of the hall was the dormitory in which I was based for my last two years. For both years I was the Coombe Court prefect and in 1959 was also Holland House Captain and School Captain of Athletics. Under normal circumstances I would have occupied the top room in the Brotherhood Hall tower in Main School, but that year another boarder, Pop Russell, was School Captain and he took precedence. Never before, and certainly never since, have I had such power over people! I can only hope that I did not abuse this power too often.

A feature of this dormitory was the French windows which opened onto a steep flight of wooden steps, lethally slippery when damp, which went down to the lawn. The steps were a favourite seat for boys using the garden. They were also a risky and unlawful short cut from the garden to the Common Room; risky because there was every chance of finding me coming the other way. The room itself held five beds and a desk on which my cases of assorted wildlife were often kept.

The foot of my bed extended halfway across a window. The wind howled in through the cracks and on one memorable occasion, when it snowed in the night, I woke to find a small snowdrift on the blanket across the end of my bed big enough for me to make a snowball! The wind howled in also through cracks in the floor if anyone had left a window open in the tuck-box room!

In spite of the Queen Mary boiler, Coombe Court had no central heating. The rest of the school was warmed by radiators, but Coombe Court had an electric 'Romany' heater in each dormitory. These tall, stove-pipe structures had a small coiled element at the base and heat rose in modest amounts from the top. Shivering boys would warm their hands over them and hold their pyjama jackets out to let warm air in before diving into bed. In winter, the first into the dormitory would switch the heater on and, unless it was bitterly cold, it was turned off at lights out. The night of the snowdrift was not cold enough for the heater to be left on - indeed the reason the snow didn't thaw was that it was insulated from my feet by my spare rug which I hadn't unfolded to use, so I cannot have felt cold!

Getting warm at bed-time in Coombe Court

The stairs up to the first floor had a large built-in cupboard on the half-landing, and in it we kept our Sunday suits. Coming onto the first floor landing, there was the bathroom straight ahead, normally used only by the resident master and the dormitory captains. It, together with the bath in the changing room, was used by the boys for their weekly bath, which was scheduled by a rota compiled by Matron, and according to which four boys had a bath each evening, first baths being at quarter past eight and second baths at half past when the main body of Coombe Court boarders were let out of prep. Anyone drawing the short straw of first bath in the changing room bath was well advised to move very swiftly and to be out of the bath, dried and, if not in bed, at least in its vicinity before the rest arrived. It was inviting trouble to be caught still in the bath when your kindly contemporaries arrived, fully clothed and mob-handed. The invitation was rarely turned down!

To the right of the bathroom was one of two upstairs toilets. The second was in the mirror-image position in the other half of the building. It was in this second toilet that the cleaning maid, Rosa, corralled a three foot grass-snake which for obvious reasons had been

66

christened Houdini by the Natural History Society. She then sought me out:

"Oh, Barker!"

"Yes, Rosa?"

"I found a serpent on the landing and thought it was something of yours."

"Is it still there?"

"No. I've put it in the toilet. I don't think it can get out. It hissed at me and it was wriggling about."

Investigation revealed that she had indeed put it in the toilet - in the lavatory pan. It was still wriggling about, and hissed at me too when I fished it out. Luckily, Rosa was a resourceful and pretty imperturbable person, who took the odd grass-snake on the first floor landing very much as a matter of course. I dread to think what would have happened if one of the other maids had found it. We had to let Houdini go shortly afterwards. We simply could not keep the thing confined to its tank and the possibility of using as a long-term home the one receptacle from which it had been unable to escape was firmly vetoed.

I've put it in the toilet.

There were no grass-snake adventures in the front toilet. Here, however, the wooden toilet seat became detached from its moorings at about the same time that first the chain and then the metal arm to which it had been attached came away. Flushing could still be achieved by standing on the lavatory pan, heaving up and pushing down the plunger. The resident master, by then the unfortunate Mr Purver, left the seat down when he attempted the exercise, and joined his own in the pan when the seat slipped, spraining his ankle in the process. Thereafter, a bucket of water was kept on standby until the dilatory plumber had carried out running repairs.

Left of the bathroom was a small dormitory with four beds. I was consigned to it for one term myself as a junior and the formidable Micky Potter was the dormitory captain. He was, like his older brother, Chris, an excellent athlete and boxer and it was a risky business waking him up if he had over slept - you were liable to be flattened in the process. The risk had to be taken because to leave him asleep was to condemn yourself to certain swift death, if you were lucky. Once, when I arrived to go to bed, I found my mattress and bed-clothes on the floor. The metal frame of my bed was being held at arm's length out of the window by Micky in the hope that one of his friends would come out of the door beneath!

If, instead of going into this small dormitory, you turned left again, it took you into one of the two larger dormitories which occupied parts of both sides of the building. The other large dormitory was to the right at the head of the stairs. They held about a dozen beds apiece and, because each was effectively two separate rooms, both had stove-pipe heaters, one for each section.

Going up to the second floor there was, again, a cupboard wardrobe on the half-landing and, at the top, four rooms. To the right was a two-bed dormitory, to the left a three-bed dormitory. From each, an emergency fire-hatch led into the other side. Beyond these were the resident master's rooms, a small bedroom to the right and a larger living room/study to the left. Joe Luker was a great fan of the Goon Show. When he invited anyone who wanted to listen to it to come to his room to do so, virtually everyone in the building joined him. Almost everybody attempted to imitate the Goons and, after a programme, Coombe Court rang to cries of: "You dirty rotten swine! You have deaded me!" and other catch phrases. The two boys occupying the smaller of the top floor dormitories were christened 'Min' and 'Henry' after the Cruns and the nickname stuck to Min Sharp from then on. Coombe Court was a complete mad-house, and it is appropriate that many of us will for ever associate it with Joe's Goon Show sessions.

Every so often we held a fire-drill for each of the residential buildings. Boys went to their dormitories and, when the fire alarms were sounded, put into practice the fire-drill for that dormitory. The fire alarms were of two kinds. The older ones were sections of four or five-inch diameter steel pipe about eighteen inches long and made of quarter-inch metal. These were suspended from brackets on the wall by wires passed through two holes bored at the top of the tube. Also suspended from the bracket, on a cord so that it hung down the centre of the tube, was a length of metal bar of about half-an-inch diameter. The end of the bar came below the end of the tube and to sound the alarm you grabbed the end of the bar and banged it back and forth across the tube. If the bar fell off, as it did sometimes, you laid into the outside of the tube with it to fine effect. The newer alarms were a foot to eighteen inches of six-inch cross-section steel H-beam. These were also suspended from brackets and hung beside them was our old friend the metal bar. These were simply bashed wherever the fancy took. The newer alarms were painted battleship grey. The tubes were merely rusty.

Coombe Court's drill was a very mundane affair. You simply walked down the stairs. Because the building had two independent stair-cases, the assumption was that so long as you could get from one side to the other you could reach a stair-case unaffected by the blaze. On the reasonable assumption that any conflagration would start in the general neighbourhood of the Queen Mary boiler, the first and second floor dormitories made their way out down the back stairs, over the wooden barrier across them. The only excitement was that the occupants of the top floor, including the resident master, had to wriggle through the fire hatches. The original fire hatches were enormously heavy and hinged at the top. The first through had to possess considerable upper body strength; the second in line was liable to have his skull flattened as the hatch swung back. Those hatches were replaced with light, side-hinged doors whose defects were that they opened by themselves in strong winds and rattled in light ones so depriving occupants of these dormitories of sleep. Home-made wooden wedges were but a partial answer to this. The ground floor dormitory simply walked down the steps from the French windows and into the garden.

The same two-staircase trick was played in Long Dorm, although sometimes they were allowed to go out of a window in Matron's Corridor and onto the bottom section of a fire escape system which led to the bedrooms of Matron, Nurse and the maids. Here they could scramble importantly down a ten-foot length of metal ladder to ground level.

Wykeham too was rather unadventurous, involving getting through fire hatches into dormitories having window-exits onto flat roofs and thence to iron ladders, or in the case of Garden Dorm hopping out of windows and into the garden.

The fun started, however, in Dormer. The ground-floor dormitory was easy. You opened the French windows and strolled out onto the path, or rather you leapt out and (O, Joy! O, Rapture!) up onto the Headmaster's lawn and amongst the rose beds to perform a key role. The first-floor dormitory nearest to The Twitten had a heavy-duty rope, about two inches in diameter. This was fixed to a strong hook by the window by means of a steel loop fixed to the rope. The loose end was cast from the window and seized by the lawn-and-rose-bed squad who held it so that it sloped down at a fairly gentle angle. The inmates then sat on the window-ledge, grasped the rope firmly, swung one leg over it, clamped that leg with the other leg and slid in a controlled manner to ground level, where they joined the anchor party. Meanwhile the second floor, including the resident master, was being evacuated down a steel-chain ladder which hung, permanently, down the side of the building. This ladder passed within inches of the side of the window of the first-floor dormitory furthest from The Twitten. The occupants of that dormitory scrambled, precariously, from their window onto it. The risk was that they would collide with those descending from on high, or, in getting onto the swinging ladder, shake off someone already on it. For fire-drills, the second-floor used it first, and the first floor second. The occupants of this first-floor dormitory had also to practice the rope trick and so had two goes. Because this operation involved desecration of the Sacred Turf, Johnny was ever-present.

Fire Drill in Dormer.

Upper Dorm had a moderately exciting time too, scrambling up a short wooden ladder onto and across the flat roof over Upper Corridor, the School Prefects' Room and Room 7, down the vertical metal ladder onto the Bog roof and then to the ground via the main fire-escape.

The *piece-de-résistance* was, however, the descent into Church Street of the Holland House Captain from the top room in the Brotherhood Hall tower. He strapped on a canvas harness attached to a steel wire rope and leapt from the window, hoping that the inertia reel on which the wire rope was wound would perform as the manufacturers claimed it would and lower him gently to the ground and neither put him into free-fall nor leave him dangling half-way down.

I have very vague memories of a canvas chute, similar to those used on aircraft and a fire-man's blanket, in fact I remember helping to hold the fireman's blanket. I think these were back-up systems for the first floor in Coombe Court, but they may have been in Wykeham.

These drills were announced in advance; always carried out in good weather; and were carefully supervised. It is interesting to speculate what would have happened if Dormer or Coombe Court had caught fire one winter's night. I have a strong suspicion that it would have gone like clockwork and that dormitory captains, prefect and resident master would have checked that no-one was missing and had everyone under cover before the fire-engine got there. Anyway, as Joe Luker pointed out, Coombe Court was so damp that you probably couldn't have ignited it even if you had wanted to.

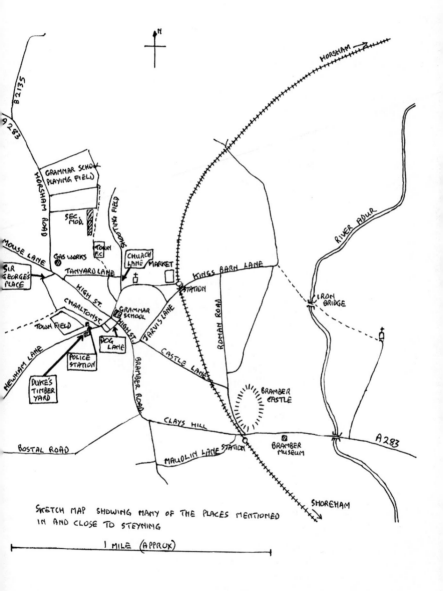

SKETCH MAP SHOWING MANY OF THE PLACES MENTIONED IN AND CLOSE TO STEYNING

1 MILE (APPROX)

73

Chapter 3

The town around us

Steyning has expanded a lot since the 1950s, although this process was already under way with the Shooting Field estate being built and some new houses in Newham Lane. The centre has changed too, but many of these changes are not immediately obvious. The shops may sell different things now - for example a small bookshop and stationers in my day is now Osborn Humphreys Estate Agents and the Co-op has been subdivided to give three different shops selling a range of goods - but they look the same superficially.

Penny Drink Shop

The two most important ones so far as the boarders were concerned have been converted into houses. One was the Tuck Shop, in Church Street, almost opposite the Brotherhood Hall entry. It was run by Mr and Mrs Cummings. He had an artificial leg and was unimaginatively called Peg-leg by us. It was here that we exchanged our pocket money and, until early 1953 when sweet rationing ended, our coupons, for sweets, crisps, tiger nuts and the other things so dear to our hearts. This is now Midsummer Cottage, but the step into the Tuck Shop, well worn by many eager feet, is still there. The other key shop in our lives was the Penny Drink Shop at the bottom of Mouse Lane. This did sell a small selection of sweets, but, as our name for it suggests, it had a carbonated water machine with which the owner could make to order a glass-full of fizzy drink for the sum of 1d. A small quantity of a flavoured and virulently coloured syrup was put in the glass and the water squirted in. You paid, drank the concoction and handed the glass back. Since it was impossible to identify the flavour you simply asked for a red, yellow or orange penny-drink. I have a terrible suspicion that there was, in addition, a green penny-drink. You could also buy single Woodbine cigarettes here and matches. Both were strictly forbidden us and had Authority known of this illicit trade, the shop would have been put out-of-bounds immediately. The Penny Drink Shop is now Windsor Cottage and the old entry in the angled corner of the building has been blocked in. The significance of these two shops was that they were the only ones we could go into after school, other than at lunchtimes on Wednesday and Saturday, without express permission.

To get permission to go and buy essentials such as ink or writing paper was not too difficult, but it was next to impossible to be allowed into places such as the Model Bakery at the junction of Sir George's Place and the High Street, in order to buy the things we craved - sticky buns, for example. However, from 1959, Johnny's father had digs in Steyning and the old man was pleased to be spoken to by the boys when meeting them in the street. He was a bit deaf and with some of the boys conversations ran along the lines:

"Good afternoon, sir!"

"Oh! Good afternoon. Going for a walk?"

"Yes, sir. Up Mouse Lane, sir." Then, *sotto voce*, "We want to buy buns from the Bakery, sir," and, loudly, "that will be all right, sir, won't it?"

This usually got a vague smile, since he had not heard everything, and the response: "Yes I'm sure it will. Have a nice walk!"

Any prefect or junior master seeing the reprobates emerging with their booty from the Bakery would be told, with truth, that Mr Scragg had said that it would be all right, omitting to mention that it was Scragg *père* and not Scragg *fils* who had unwittingly given his blessing to the enterprise.

Any of the members of staff in my time would see a dramatic reduction in the number of pubs. These were of no real interest to us, since we would not have been served there, but simply reported. Even the most senior boys usually looked outside the town if they wanted to sneak a beer. Some of the staff seemed to reckon it a duty to patrol the pubs, sampling their wares as they did so, just to make sure that the bars were not filled with small boys wearing school ties and caps. Gone now are The George, opposite Mouse Lane at its junction with the High Street, The Soldiers Return, in Charlton Street opposite the Athletics Club, The Three Tuns, in the High Street almost opposite Springwells, and The Railway Inn. Being so close to the school, The Norfolk Arms was the 'local' for many staff - although The Three Tuns was also used. Johnny, tactfully, used The White Horse - sometimes The Chequer. The Norfolk featured in a song to the tune Cwm Rhondda often sung by boarders:

'We are going to have a party
What a party it will be!
There will be provision in plenty,
Lots of goodies we will see.
Bread of heaven,
Cheese from Devon,
Beer from The Norfolk Arms (Norfolk Arms),
Beer from The Norfolk Arms.'

Cardiff Arms Park (sorry, the National Stadium, Cardiff!) would have been proud of us.

A place of great significance to many day boys, as well as boarders, and which is no more, was the railway station. Rail was the easiest way of getting to and from places such as Portslade, Shoreham and Lancing. Many boarders travelled by train to and from home too. On Wednesday afternoons in the summer, it was the Steyning Stinker which huffed and puffed to Hove with, under Digger's supervision, those in that week's select group going swimming at the King Alfred Baths.

The traffic was two way, though, and girls from Steyning travelled north each day to Horsham High School, returning around half-past-four. It was always surprising how many boys found urgent business in the general vicinity of the station at about the time the girls' train got in!

The station was the entry-port for a lot of goods destined for businesses in Steyning and the place from which produce was sent out. The cattle market had a strong symbiotic relationship with the station and was also popular with the boarders. The market was held on Wednesdays, when we had a half-day and a shopping break before lunch. There was a fish and chip van parked always in Station Road, by the way into the market, and we were allowed, if we wished, to buy 3d or 6d bags of chips. Matron was never entirely convinced about our eating chips before we had lunch, and was rather doubtful about the standards of hygiene, but we were pretty well immune by then to most bacteria!

Apart from the chips, it was great fun looking at the chickens, geese, ducks, rabbits, sheep, goats, cattle and pigs. The pigs, especially, could be guaranteed for a laugh as people tried to drive them up ramps into trucks, or when a little one escaped into the crowd, its passage marked by curses and squeals and a slight swaying of the throng as though an otter were passing through a reed-bed. Then, on one momentous occasion, an enterprising fourteen-year-old bid for and, with the full connivance of the auctioneer and audience of grinning farmers, acquired, a piglet. It was given a good deal of attention when brought back to school, however, neither Glubbie nor Johnny were swayed by the plausible argument that, by using waste from the school kitchen, financial gain could be made. The piglet was returned to the arena *ek dum* and the auctioneer given unambiguous instruction that under no circumstances whatsoever were livestock, deadstock, machinery or job-lots from the sale-field to be sold to boarders, no matter what the law of the land said, or did not say, on the matter. The boy concerned was not punished. The reprimand was along the lines that rearing a piglet involved more time than the boy could devote to it and that, although input to the animal had been thought out well, output from it had been inadequately considered. Johnny liked to see enterprise!

It was given a good deal of attention..........

Also in the station area at the junction of Kings Barn Villas with Kings Barn Lane was the Steyning Steam Laundry which dealt with our laundry. When it eventually burned down it was demolished. This laundry was on the edge of the railway cutting just to the Bramber side of the station and by a road bridge over the railway. When a junior, I well remember standing on this bridge to watch the train leave the station and pass under us. Apart from the thrill of watching, we tried to drop pebbles down the funnel. The driver and fireman were always ready for us though, and made sure we got a really good blast of soot and clinkers as they went under the bridge. The advantage of the Steyning Stinker was that it was very noisy. It was also pretty slow. The risk to us therefore was minimal when we looked for slow-worms and adders on the embankments, or put ha'pennies to be squashed on the line on the un-manned crossing in Castle Lane on the walk to Bramber Castle. The driver and fireman would simply smile and wave to us. It never occurred to us to try to obstruct the line, or play games with the trains, and I remember our indignation when vandals near Horsham once put a sleeper on the line.

Another source of great wonder and interest was Duke's timber yard in Newham Lane. You could stand in the lane or on the raised footpath and watch the men barring tree trunks onto the trolley and running the huge butts lengthwise through the band-saw to cut planks. I loved the rumble of the trolley and the scream and power of the saw. We used to watch for minutes on end before someone would remind us, eventually, that we were trying to get onto the Downs.

Duke's timber yard

Although, by the time I arrived, the tan-yard had closed (we were often told about the smell which wafted from it across the town) another source of smell, the gas works, was going strong. Chemistry classes learning about coal gas manufacture were taken round it, but by the time that I had reached this stage in my education, the works had closed. My recollection is that you got into it from a road which joined the Horsham Road just past The George. There were big and rather ugly metal gates across this road.

The 1950s schoolboy would find places such as the Steyning Centre, Library and Museum an improvement on the facilities we enjoyed, and the range of facilities and occupations which the vastly enlarged school provides, mouth-watering. However, *for the schoolboy boarder*'I think more has been lost from the town than has been gained and the pastimes which we enjoyed were the better for being hard-won by our own endeavours and crafted from the extraordinary range of possibilities the area held - if you used your imagination and behaved responsibly - well *reasonably* responsibly. I can *never* remember being bored in my free time.

Chapter 4

Appearance and behaviour

We had to appear neat and tidy at all times, and school uniform was compulsory for everyone during school hours and for boarders at all times. The uniform was a light blue blazer with the school badge on it, a plain, navy blazer with silver buttons for VI Formers, or a grey herring-bone, light tweed jacket. Trousers were grey flannel shorts or long trousers. Shirts for juniors were light grey, long-sleeved cotton or, in the summer, a dark blue Airtex short-sleeved one. White shirts were worn by senior boys and by all boarders on Sundays. Many day boys and some junior boarders wore white shirts every day. A school tie had to be worn, except in very hot weather after an official announcement had been made that you could take off your jacket and tie in school. Both had to be put on again to leave the school and go into the town. They could be taken off again only once you were away from the houses. Of course, boarders regularly took off ties, jackets and caps once up on the Downs, whatever the weather, but were careful to put them back on before reaching town again. Each of the four Houses had its own distinctive 'colours' tie and anyone who had been awarded their 'colours' would almost always wear that tie in preference to the red-white-and-blue-striped school tie. The VI Formers could wear a plain, pale blue tie as an alternative to the school tie. We kept our ties neatly pressed by winding them round the cylindrical bar of the bed-frame's foot at night. Long grey socks, with the school colours round the top, had to be worn with shorts and with long trousers, grey socks - although you could get away then with any dark colour. Shoes were black and there was some latitude given in terms of style, but not a lot. Brown sandals were also allowed in the summer. In colder weather, a grey sleeveless or long-sleeved sweater with the school colours round the base could be worn under your jacket. In wet weather, navy-blue rain-coats were the prescribed wear.

81

Black Wellington boots were on the boarders' list of required clothes too.

On Sunday mornings, boarders had to put on white shirts, plain black ties and grey Sunday suits and, unless it was decreed otherwise, overcoats had to be worn or carried to church. The first thing you did when you got back from church was to go to your dormitory to take off and hang up suits and overcoats, and change into your every-day gear.

The uniform was obtainable only from Messrs Cobleys in Hove. Boarders were given a clothes list of what should be brought each term, and how many of each. This ensured a degree of uniformity, but also allowed for some variety. This variety was most evident in the towels and, oddly, the under-pants provided by parents for their off-spring. Where, for example in my own case, parents could ill-afford to buy new clothes for us, the occasionally used items, such as 'a grey suit' and 'a white shirt' for Sundays, were not those sold by Messrs Cobleys, but hand-downs from older brothers or cousins. They differed in style, colour and texture from those worn by the majority. In cold weather, a similarly non-conforming overcoat was added to my Sunday sartorial torment. The embarrassment and misery caused to me in my first year by being the only boy in the school who had white shirts with separate collars - which called for all too easily lost front and back collar studs - was acute. I dreaded Sundays all through my first year for this reason alone. On Sunday, the normal range of personal inspections was supplemented by a church parade inspection by the Housemaster or Headmaster. Both were understanding enough not to add to my plight by making any comment other than the standard: "Pull your socks up!" which seemed to be a conditioned reflex in Authority to even the briefest glimpse of me.

Finally, out of school, we all had to wear light blue caps with the school badge on the front. Custom dictated that the further you rose in the school, the further to the back of the head your cap migrated. By the VI Form, a cap which had been worn in your first year with its peak horizontal and square to the front over your eyes, had become a beanie on the back of the head, with its peak distinctly off-square to the right and at an angle of forty-five degrees to the horizontal. House Prefects had a red trim on the back half of their caps. School Prefects had this bright red trim all the way round. Seen from the front, a School Prefect appeared to be wearing a slightly skewed red halo. This was useful warning colouration so far as juniors were concerned. Caps *had* to be worn outside school, even if you were only crossing Church Street to the Tuck Shop. This was strictly enforced anywhere

Meeting a master in the street

in the town, in other villages, or along roads. Once onto the Downs, we usually stuffed our caps into our pockets, but hastily resumed them if a master or prefect hove into sight.

In the town, boys were expected to *walk*, especially in the High Street. When you met any townsfolk, you had to move towards the kerb side of the pavement and go single file to pass them. If necessary you stepped off into the road to do so. You were not supposed to shout across the road or down the street to each other. You could exercise the rights of H.M. subjects to 'pass and re-pass upon the highway', but in doing so everyone, but everyone, had priority over you. On meeting any member of staff outside school, boys were expected to raise their caps, although it was normally sufficient just to touch the peak. This applied even in The Twitten should you be wearing your cap going out on, or returning from, a walk. Any masters' wives you recognised got the same treatment, together with a polite 'Good morning' or 'Good afternoon', followed by their name. Mrs Scragg and Mrs Gooderson were our 'usuals'.

Staff were always addressed as 'Sir' (or 'Miss Sage' in the case of Freda Sage!). The caretakers and groundsman as Mr Nash, Mr Savage, Mr Newman or Mr Hawes. The caterer was also addressed by name - Miss Agate and then, on Aggie's retirement, Mrs Barnes - but Matron always was 'Matron' and Nurse was 'Nurse'. The maids, who helped in the kitchen and cleaned the houses were called by their first names, May, Margaret, Mary, Rosa and so on.

All boys were called by their surnames by everyone. With your personal friends you often would use first names or nicknames, but other than that, whatever use you made of nicknames when talking about someone to your friends, you reverted to the surname when addressing them, even in private. A conversation might be going on below me in the Coombe Court tuck-box room along the lines:

"Are we allowed up the field before breakfast tomorrow?"

"I don't know. Ask Beetle."

"No. Go on. You ask him."

"All right. Just because you're scared!"

But when the knock came on the door the nick-name had vanished.

"Please, Barker! Are we allowed up the field before breakfast tomorrow?" and my response that I would have to ask Glubbie, when I actually put the request, mutated to:

"Please, Sir! Can a small group of us go up the field early tomorrow?"

Staff used surnames when they knew them. Most, if not all, also adopted the useful generic term 'boy', used normally in the vocative (but sometimes, to our ears at least, in the accusative or the abusive!) as in 'Boy! Stop running in the corridor!'; 'Boy! Come *here* boy!'; 'Boy! What are you doing, boy?'; 'Boy! Pull up your socks!' This had the advantage of halting in their tracks anyone within earshot and nipping in the bud untold numbers of unsuspected misdemeanours.

When a teacher came into the classroom, all talking stopped and everyone stood up. The standard response from the master was: "All right! Sit!"; "Sit!"; or a gesture of the hand similar to that of a conductor seeking a *diminuendo* from the orchestra. If another adult - a member of staff, a care-taker, Matron or whoever - came into the room while a class was being held, or into prep, everyone stood up and remained standing until told to sit by the interloper or by the person in charge. The exception to this was a PE lesson in full swing, where most of us were on our feet in any case. On grounds of safety, Shocker would usually get us 'standing easy' or lined up and running on the spot, before finding out the reason for the intrusion. In the labs, woodwork and art rooms, the formalities were slightly relaxed, although we were supposed to stop banging bits of wood with mallets and chisels, or whatever we were doing, and to cause no back-of-the-class explosions, violent electrical short-circuits etc while the visitor was there.

When it came to personal hygiene, day boys were left to their own devices. Boarders were not. With every justification, it was suspected that your average eleven to fifteen-year-old boy, well away from parental gaze, would set their standards of neatness and cleanliness, of both clothes and person, a tad lower than that thought desirable by adults. Therefore, immediately before breakfast and high tea, the prefects inspected everyone except VI Formers. You stood by your place at table, with your back to it, and the prefects walked along the lines. The three standard targets were hair, hands (back and front), and shoes (also back and front), but crooked ties, muddy trousers, grubby faces or anything else of this kind that caught the eye were fair game too. Those failing to pass muster had to leave the dining hall to make the defect good. This was serious, because you lost out on valuable eating time. In breakfast inspections, there was little excuse for not passing - unless you had left it late getting up and skimped combing your hair, or, in the case of first-years, had fallen over in the playground. (This latter because first-years were always forced to get up immediately the rising bell went and so usually had time to kill. Most others were 'given' ten minutes by the dormitory captain.) The tea inspection was a different matter! Getting a shine on black shoes and mud off grey trousers after spending an hour with friends in a damp and muddy chalk pit is not easy. The grime of the day had to be dealt with on hands and under nails and, if you had been messing about with glue, oil, paint and the other contaminants associated with the construction, flying and destruction of model aeroplanes this too was a challenge.

Getting ready for inspection

Before lights-out, dormitory captains would inspect, ruthlessly, any suspected of skimping washing - necks and between toes being the usual targets. After your weekly bath, inspection was mandatory and normally carried out by the resident member of staff or building prefect, except in Main School where Matron subjected Long Dorm inmates to scrutiny.

Our clothes were dealt with more cursorily, other than for visible exterior mud. Once a week, on Saturday, Matron and Nurse sorted out bundles of clean clothes for all the boarders. These were set out, alphabetically by initial letter of the surname, on beds in Long Dorm. Each consisted of: a pair of pants; a vest; a pair of socks; a white shirt; a grey shirt; a handkerchief; a pillow-case; a sheet; a dirty-linen bag; and the ensemble wrapped round with a towel, tucked neatly into itself to keep all together. You collected these between morning school and tea.

The equivalent set of dirties was put in the dirty-linen bag, kept under your bed until Monday morning and then taken by you and piled up in a heap in Long Dorm. Matron and Nurse then sorted everything into the laundry baskets and the minions of the Steyning Steam Laundry were summoned to take these away and to do their worst. Matron and Nurse also dealt with the consignment on return, repairing ours and the laundry's damage where possible, sorting everyone's possessions out into their own piles in the clothes cupboard and pursuing, with imprecations, items lost, stolen or strayed within the laundry's walls.

Should some calamity occur in the week - I recall burning the foot off a sock when I tried to dry it rapidly on the boiler, and a towel made impossibly muddy when it, together with the gym kit rolled up in it, were dropped into a trench dug in the playground by workmen - you could ask Matron for a replacement and, unlike the sock, you were advised to be fire-proof if you did so. Many boys preferred to try to rectify the damage themselves, often making matters infinitely worse. I refer you again to my sock!

During the 1950s, the country was emerging from the short-back-and-sides haircuts of previous years and was moving towards more adventurous styles. Some were deemed too adventurous for us and although a few day boys managed to get away with Teddy Boy DAs and quiffs, boarders could not. Thanks to war movies, many yearned for an American crew-cut, partly because it was admired, but partly because it was the essential launch-pad for any of the longer-haired 'stand up' styles. Crew cuts were also banned and there were frightful scenes when Tommy Thompson persuaded the local barber to give him one. It appeared that having a crew-cut ranked fourth after sex, smoking and drinking alcohol on the school's list of deadly sins. It certainly ranked higher than murder and mayhem!

To keep us properly shorn, the local barber, Arthur Cassie, visited the school once a week in the evening (I seem to recall it being on Thursday) and set up shop in the washroom by Upper Dorm in the Brotherhood Hall tower. Three or four boys 'on the list' for haircuts were summoned and, as soon as one was 'done' he returned to prep to summon a replacement, until Arthur declared no more that night. He had the usual barber's collection of ribald stories and jokes and kept us well-entertained.

Arthur Cassie also drove the Steyning fire engine. On several occasions the fire-siren sounded in the middle of a haircut. Arthur would then drop everything - literally - and sprint off down the High Street to get the fire-engine under way. Someone would pick up and set aside the tools of his trade, sweep up the clippings, and return the unshorn and partly shorn to prep. The form was that the half-done victim presented himself at the earliest opportunity at the salon in the High Street to be finished. This could also happen during the day to customers from the town. Everyone knew of this possibility and everyone understood if they saw someone wandering about with a short-back-and-sides to the right of the head and badly in need of a trim to the left.

No matter how polite, clean, tidy and shorn, no boarder was allowed to visit home without express permission, even if home was as close as Shoreham. If you wanted leave to go home at the weekend, you had to present your request in person to the Holland Housemaster, and it had to be supported by a letter from home. It was quite difficult to get permission, but I remember succeeding once when my mother asked for my services to help her get in a bumper crop of apples!

Every so often there was a leave weekend when there was no school on Saturday morning. Anyone who wanted to go home could do so, or go to stay with a friend's family. You left on Friday after school and returned in time for tea on Sunday. The small residue left in school contracted into one dormitory in each building, sometimes two if there was not enough room in one. We all mucked in in the kitchen at breakfast, with boys and staff doing the cooking and washing up. We played games, went for walks, watched television, listened to records or read in the evenings and did not have to go to church on Sunday. Bliss!

On top of this there was, of course, the half term break. Most went home or stayed with a friend, but once, in the summer term of 1959, when my parents were living in Switzerland, I took a train to Exeter and set off to walk over Exmoor to the coast of the Bristol Channel and then back via Dartmoor. My equipment was: one rucksack (borrowed from a master); assorted clothes; one blanket; one cycling cape; one tin of baked beans; a pen-knife; a plastic plate; a school knife, fork and spoon; a tin mug; and about £5 in cash. I walked nearly twenty miles the evening I arrived, drank too much cider in a pub, and bedded down in a small copse beside the road. Next morning I awoke in a marsh, with a very surprised cow gazing down at me. Why I did not die of exposure on Exmoor the following night I will never know. I had been unable to get further supplies, it being Sunday, and my beans had been eaten for supper. I had the sense to get up and keep walking, and reached the warmth, food and safety of Weston-super-Mare a good day before I had meant to. On the way back, I gave up after a night on Dartmoor and hitched a lift back to Exeter. We were stopped almost at once by a police road-block! There had been a break-out from Princeton in the night! I got back to school a day early and had to burgle Coombe Court (opening one of the classroom windows with a school knife), and camped in my dormitory until the rest appeared. Johnny enquired in jocular fashion where I had been on the night of the jail-break and was a bit startled when I told him I had been about five miles from the prison, sleeping rough!

This sort of behaviour was supported by the school, although never thrust on you. I was nineteen by then, after all, and just off to university. It was seen as character building, but I imagine that had a junior expressed a wish to have done this he would have been told that an adult had to be with him.

You kept in touch with your parents by letter. Boarders were obliged, at a minimum, to write home each week on Sunday. Letter writing took place after breakfast and before church. Letters were never read by staff, but it was, on rare occasions, suggested (almost always via the Holland House Captain) that it would be wise to play down a particular event. However, the boys seemed to agree amongst themselves, almost without discussion, what was to be kept from parents and what was not. Having completed your letter, you addressed and sealed the envelope, wrote your name in the top right-hand corner and posted it in a wooden letter-box at the back of Big School in the alcove below the war memorial. A prefect emptied the box, put a stamp over your name and ticked you off on the register. This had the double function of checking that you had written home and recording expenditure to be transferred to the bill sent to parents. Letters could be written and mailed in this way at any time, not just on Sundays.

To underpin the rules and regulations, were sanctions. These ranged from the gentle reprimand: "Don't do that!", to expulsion. I can only recall one boy being excluded permanently. Although in 1951 the school prefects and staff could cane boys, this was changed almost immediately after I arrived so that only the Headmaster and the four Housemasters could use the cane. The Headmaster could beat any boy; Housemasters only boys in their House. Resident masters in Main School, Dormer, Wykeham and Coombe Court could not beat boys and crimes which in their view merited physical punishment were referred to the Housemaster. Paradoxically, the dormitory captains could beat boys, but only with a bedroom slipper. The building prefect could slipper anyone in that building; the other dormitory captains only those from their own dormitories who committed crimes within those dormitories, for example, talking after lights-out. The slipper was reserved for domestic matters in the building of residency and no prefect could use physical punishment for other offences in school or off school premises. No-one, from Headmaster to dormitory captain, could give anyone more than six whacks on the bottom - no other target was permitted - and for most offences two, three or four were the norm. I only got six once, and that was from Johnny and well-deserved. I was seen throwing stones from the top of Coombe Court garden onto the roof of the tiled shed at the bottom of the garden, thereby breaking tiles as well as rules.

Slippered for talking after lights-out

In fact, boys were not beaten on a really regular basis and the practice became less usual as time went by. This certainly applied to caning. When I left it was still quite common for boys to be slippered.

For academic failure, or some misdemeanours in class, the staff could keep boys back after school for a period of detention. This was 'booked' for a day or so after being imposed so that the parents of day boys could be warned that their son would be later home than usual that day. No-one liked to be kept in DT, although I remember accepting it in preference to an uncomfortable encounter with Jonah when given the option, but you tried harder to avoid being kept in by some masters than others. For some it was sufficient to deprive a boarder of his liberty, or to make sure that a day boy had to catch a bus or train an hour later than usual. By these you might be told simply to read a book. Others, like Mr Blackaby, devised interesting ways of giving extra tuition and were with you throughout to help and discuss. Many, in effect, gave you extra prep with little or no help offered.

Common punishments from prefects for 'in hours' misdemeanours were learning a hymn by heart, writing 'lines' or, more imaginatively, 'sides'. Lines were the traditional "Write out one hundred times 'I must not run in Upper Corridor'." Sides tested the sadistic ingenuity of the prefect concerned: "Write me two-sides on 'worms' by lights-out tomorrow". Or it could be on Don Quixote, flint axes, Sanskrit, evolution, or whatever took the fancy. This at least demanded some constructive research in the library, although you were well-advised not to copy chunks from the Encyclopaedia Britannica, since this risked a repeat exercise. School prefects could punish any boy in this way, and for a boarder to be given lines or sides by a day boy prefect was seen as a particular disgrace by his peers. House prefects could only punish directly those in their own House, but they could refer the criminal up the chain of command to a School Prefect or Housemaster. Although a prefect could refer someone direct to the Headmaster, this was almost never done. The Housemaster was the normal referee and would have been put out had someone by-passed him.

For boarders, there were other sanctions. You could be gated for a period, be given jobs to do after school, such as cleaning the playground, or be sent on punishment runs. These runs were usually short - round the bottom of the Horseshoe if you were lucky; round the top if you were not. If the prefect concerned was not a keen runner himself you could dawdle, within reason (as in: "Please, Hopkins! My shoe kept falling off."), take short cuts, or simply run briskly up Sheep Pen Lane and then veer down Charlton Street to the Mill Field to have a crafty smoke or simply talk to friends for fifteen minutes. You then set off back to school at speed, treading in such mud or puddles as you could find, to arrive breathless and mud-splashed after the right interval of time, having covered a quarter of a mile instead of the two and a half or three and a half miles expected of you. Of course, if you were unlucky, the prefect concerned was the House Cross Country Captain and came too. This meant you running, running all the way, running fast, and suffering.

Punishment run - running fast and suffering...

Inconsistency in both staff and prefects in meting out punishment was detested. Severity was not enjoyed, but was greatly preferred to inconsistency. With some, such as Jonah or Slopey Joe, you knew you were for it if caught, but you also knew that the same crime would get the same punishment every time, no matter who was committing it. With others you never knew whether you would be let off lightly one day for a major sin and punished severely for a lesser transgression the next. As a senior prefect, I often had to comfort juniors in tears, not over the punishment itself, but the unfairness of the inconsistency in its application. On several occasions I had to intercede on their behalf with the master concerned, and was driven twice to speak to the Headmaster.

As a prefect, you had to acquire certain skills, known these days as 'man-management skills', if you were to survive and be respected. Some prefects could quell a riot simply by appearing in the door. Others made matters worse by their presence. All prefects had to be able to get the whole school quiet before morning Assembly and Holland House prefects had the added ordeals of Names and prep supervision.

In morning assembly, the duty prefect reading the lesson collected the Bible from the Headmaster's study, took it down to the gym, went in by the door nearest the stage, on which was the lectern, and mounted the stage. The school was by now lined up across the gym in forms, everyone chatting merrily and noisily to his neighbours. There were prefects stationed between each form, backs to the wall-bars, and they made sure that no high-jinks occurred within each form and between different forms. They were little help to the duty prefect in getting hush! Up on the stage, if I was duty prefect, I would take my time finding the place in the Bible and would read through the passage concerned - or pretend to. Then, a minute before the staff were due to file onto the stage from the changing room, I would walk to the centre of the stage to stand beside the Headmaster's table, take a deep breath and yell: "STOP TALKING!!!" at the top of my voice and pitching it to the VI Form at the back. Immediately, the buzz of conversation died down, but, if you were not careful, having died to a low point, it began to pick up again. As soon as I detected the turning point, I would locate someone in the middle ranks of the school whose name I knew and who was still talking: "ROBSON!! Come and stand in front of 2B!" This meant reporting to the

Headmaster after Assembly and having the acute embarrassment of standing, like a giant, in front of a row of pygmies and under the disinheriting gaze of Johnny and the entire staff. It was totally unfair and worked like a charm. I was very grateful to Stinge Smith for giving me the tip when I was made a prefect. If you picked a first or second year, they were too junior to have an impact. If you picked someone in Remove or the VI Form you risked outright mutiny or an argument between the back of the audience - by now a highly amused and appreciative audience - and the stage. Remove 2 were too junior to argue, but senior enough to be a lesson and a warning. Since it was the boarders whose names I knew best, it was usually an R2 boarder who carried the can. Reporting to Johnny merely meant a telling off, but, even so, I did apologise to the victim on several occasions and made sure he got some compensation, such as putting him down to watch television.

Prep and Names were Holland House affairs and here you were relieved of the presence of VI Formers. The rest could give you quite enough trouble! Again, talking was the usual crime and, especially in Senior Prep, it was surprisingly difficult to identify the culprit. My technique was to pick on the person I was reasonably confident was guilty and invite them to see me after prep. That gave me time to devise excruciating punishment and them time to prepare their case. At all events, it postponed noisy argument until the time most of the others had gone. I remember once asking a boy in Remove called Simon Dannatt (Splat) to do me a couple of sides for talking.

"But, Barker! I wasn't talking and shouldn't be punished. It isn't fair!"

"Look, I'm not interested in that. Someone was talking and I think it was you. If it wasn't, then it is up to you to take it out on whoever it was."

Pause for consideration:

"OK," rushing out of the door and down the corridor: "QUINLAN!!"

The next evening Splat handed in his two sides, neat and well-researched, but in a hand not his own. A hand which closely resembled that of his friend, and, I am pleased to say, still a friend of mine, Tony Quinlan.

Marbled white butterfly on round-headed rampion

Chapter 5

An educational progression

Between the first year and Remove, the school was divided into an 'A' stream and a 'B' stream. The 'A' stream held the more academically inclined. In each class there were between twenty-five and thirty-five boys. You rose in the school by age, rather than by academic achievement, and so moved inexorably upward over five years towards 'O' Levels, which were taken in Remove. As 'O' Levels were neared, there were some opportunities to choose between different subjects to take for the exams - the choice between geography and Latin being one that I have mentioned already.

Most people in the 'A' stream sat the exams in nine subjects. In my case these were: English language; English literature; history; French; Latin; maths; physics; chemistry; and biology. Many boys left school at this point, but an increasing number stayed then for another three years to specialise and take 'A' and 'S' Levels. There were the VI Forms to cater for this and from Remove you moved into the Lower VI and thence, through the VI to the Upper VI. It was normal to take three subjects at the end of your second year in the VI Form, mine being botany, zoology, and chemistry, but if you were taking 'S' Level sciences you had to pass a use of English exam. This was not a separate qualification but had to be passed before 'S' Levels were awarded. Everyone took a general knowledge paper and this was an 'O' Level qualification. The Biology VI in my year voted to sit 'O' Level botany to keep our hands in at 'proper' exams and so picked up an extra 'O' in the process.

Johnny had a special interest in the general knowledge paper and it was a class he taught himself. In my time, the VI Form class was held in Penfold Church Hall. He felt we should have a broad range of interests and, I felt, rather regretted the specialisation demanded by 'A' Levels. I remember him setting the whole school a general knowledge test one term, to which all the staff had contributed questions. He was absolutely horrified at the depth of our ignorance, and spoke long and eloquently to the whole school about it at Assembly. One of my contemporaries, by that time in the Maths VI, reduced Shocker to a state of helpless giggles. In marking papers he found that, when invited to fill the blank in: "------ to make and the match to win", the boy had contributed: "A fag to make and the match to win". I hardly think that Simon Pascoe was unfamiliar with Sir Henry Newbolt's jingoistic masterpiece, but he had obviously found the opportunity for a bit of fun too good to miss.

The normal school day began with Assembly at nine. This was followed by two forty-five minute periods, after which was a twenty minute play break. There were then two more forty-five minute periods before lunch. In the afternoon, we had three more periods and school finished at twenty-to-four. Wednesdays and Saturdays were half days and school ended at twelve, after we had sat through four periods of forty minutes. It was this early finish which gave boarders the hour before lunch in which to go shopping.

For boarders, each weekday ended with two prep periods, one either side of the evening prayers break at seven. Although we had an advantage over day boys, in that these periods gave no chance to give way to temptations to skimp prep, and ensured that we could work without distraction, there was the disadvantage that it was hard to get help if you got stuck. You could ask the duty master or prefect to help; some would, some would not. For someone like me, it was no use anybody asking for help with their maths. It would only make matters worse! It was noticeable, however, that boarders did better, relatively, in exams - when no-one got helped - than in marks for prep!

In prep you were not allowed to talk or to read a novel without permission. Junior Prep, in Big School, was supervised by the duty master and all staff were on a rota to oversee boarders' tea, take the roll call, and then first prep. At the end of first prep, juniors simply stood by the desks they had been working on, the duty master left, the seniors and prefects came in and stood at the back and the Holland Housemaster came in to lead prayers. The second prep for juniors was supervised by a prefect. Senior Prep was supervised throughout by a prefect, and the prefects were themselves doing school work too. The difficulties for a prefect - assuming he had no general problems in keeping discipline - came in junior second prep. Starting around half-past seven, you risked getting immersed in what you were doing and over-shooting an eight o'clock mark of high significance for two first-years. There would be a clearing of throats and you would look up to see a couple of anxious faces and two arms aloft: "Please, Barker! Can the eight o'clock baths go?"

Can the eight o'clock baths go?

Then fifteen minutes later, it was time for the rest of the first years to vanish and the first baths for Coombe Court and Dormer. Simultaneously, you hoped, the duty prefect in Senior Prep would release the Long Dorm dormitory captain, thus preventing a riot in Long Dorm. At half past eight all the juniors were liberated. It was hard for a prefect to concentrate on his own work in junior second prep!

If boys genuinely had finished all their prep, and it was not near the end of term school exams, they were usually given permission to read a novel, provided it was to hand. Having it to hand, in the hope that you would have finished your prep and be allowed to read it, was a temptation in itself. The sight of a boy apparently gazing intently at his groin was a sure sign that temptation had proved too much!

"Stone! Bring that book up here!

"What is it? Ah, splendid! *Treasure Island*. Do me two sides on 'parrots' by prep tomorrow."

The temptation was the stronger since permission to read was by no means always given. Certainly, near exams, the request was invariably met with: "Haven't you any revision to do? Get on with that. You can read after the exams."

With limited resources, the school was stretched when it came to staff and in junior classes and some 'B' stream classes in particular, you found staff teaching the rudiments of subjects which were not the ones they specialised in. Thus Shocker was found teaching English, since Percy Coltman could not teach Remove and 2B simultaneously and Joe Luker seen keeping one lesson ahead of the class in 'B' stream chemistry. Joe's chemistry classes were far more entertaining than Buffer Bennett's ever were. Just after he had got engaged to Hilary Gooderson, his prospective father-in-law was in Room 5 teaching maths to the 'A' stream of our year. Immediately below him, Joe was demonstrating the preparation of hydrogen to a 'B' stream class. The murmur from below hardly impinged upon us, but a sudden explosion and the sound of tinkling glass certainly did. Maths came to a temporary halt. Joe's voice rose like a sea-gull above the waves of hubbub: "Is everyone OK? ... Good! Right, someone get another set of apparatus out of the cupboard and I'll try again!"

After a decent pause during which there was still an excited hum from the class, Joe's voice rose again:

"Right! Everybody down!!"

BANG!! ... tinkle, tinkle!

"Right! You two help pick up the bits. The rest go into the playground." Glubbie was by this time bouncing up and down nervously and expressing to us the hope that 'John is all right'. Buffer was airborne on his way to prevent the total demolition of his lab, and to teach his apprentice how to ensure that the hydrogen was no longer in an explosive mixture with air inside the apparatus before lighting the stream of gas to demonstrate that water was formed. Amazingly, absolutely no-one was injured by flying glass or acid!

Right! Everybody down!!

Every three weeks, the marks for prep and class work for that period were totted up for every class up to Remove 1. The results were ranked, a class order produced by the form-master and passed to Johnny. At Assembly, the Three-Weekly Order was read to the school. He began with 2B and worked up the school. He also read the lists in reverse order, so, in my class, we usually began: "Thirty-three, Barker, G." and finished: "First, Russell". When I was in Remove 3, or possibly even in Remove 2, my parents got a little concerned about my permanent residence in the basement of the class and discussed it with Johnny. He asked them to leave the matter with him and he would investigate what was wrong. His first line of approach was to invite me to wait upon him in his study at my earliest possible convenience - like immediately. He then reviewed my position in class over the successive three-weekly orders since the beginning of time, and gave me his sincere and most binding promise that, unless there was a marked and prompt improvement in my academic performance, he would beat me. By strange coincidence, I came sixth in the following three-weekly order before slipping, gradually, to a position more comfortable in terms of effort, but not so comfortable as to be conspicuous - say between twentieth and twenty-fifth. Having noted this, Johnny wrote to my parents saying that they need not be worried; the ability was there and was applied intelligently, provided the interest and motivation were there too. His analysis was that I would do enough to get by - just - unless something really interested me, or unless the imminence of external exams, or threats of a more direct nature, provided the stimulus. How accurate that assessment was! This was said of me, rather more obliquely, in a valedictory speech when I retired in June 2000! It was at this ceremony that I discovered, for the first time, what was said in the reference given to me by the University of Oxford when I applied for my job - it was the same again!

While progress was assessed by prep, tests in class, class-work and end of term exams, none of this contributed to external exam gradings. These were quite independent of course-work marks and, because some people got very tense when the 'O' and 'A' Level exams came round, they probably scored lower than they would had course-work been included in the assessment. However, we were all conditioned to this 'one off' system. We normally sat the Cambridge Examination Board exams, but when in my year we decided to take 'O' Level botany as part of our VI Form work, we sat an Oxford exam because Cambridge set no botany 'O' Level syllabus.

It is usual now to take a year out between finishing school and going to university. My year was the first, I think, (but possibly the second) to miss compulsory National Service, which lasted eighteen months. Here was, in effect, a year out which everyone took. When I went from Steyning to Oxford, the dons were outraged and concerned that, whereas in the past they had an intake of young men, they were now getting schoolboys. Those dons, at least, would have approved most heartily the idea of a year out!

In addition to regular class work, VI Formers in particular could get approval to go to outside lectures, concerts or plays. In my time in the Biology VI we went to Brighton to hear a lecture on dinosaurs by Dr Swinton, a well-known expert. We also went to a series of WEA evening lectures, held in the school, which was about flowers, their taxonomy and identification. Most memorable of all, was a trip to the Dome in Brighton to hear a concert conducted by Sir Thomas Beecham. Some fools came in late, just as he raised his baton and we were treated to one of Sir Thomas's exhibitions of silent contempt, disgust and loathing as the latecomers slunk into their seats under his glacial stare. The piece we had gone to hear was Beethoven's violin concerto. Before the concert began, a gentleman appeared on the conductor's rostrum to make an announcement. He regretted that the young solo violinist due to perform for us was unwell. Our hearts sank - all that expense and travelling and we were going to miss what we had come for. However, he continued, the violinist's teacher and mentor had heard about this and was going to play in his stead. That teacher was Yehudi Menhuin!! How lucky can you get! He was at the height of his powers then and, had the concert been advertised with him as soloist, we would not have had a snowball's chance in hell of getting tickets.

I went once to see *Macbeth*, as played by my brother's school, Christs Hospital. Housey has its own railway station and so it was a door-to-door trip on the Steyning Stinker. Alas, I reached the station, having seen and enjoyed the play, just as the last train left. It meant a hike of a good sixteen miles, which got me back to Coombe Court at about two in the morning. In the High Street, I did the comedy classic of bumping into a lamp-post and apologising to it, with the policeman about six feet away who had heard me coming and had slipped into a shop doorway to find out who I was. Need I say that he found the whole situation amusing? I did not!

Apologising to the lamp-post.

Chapter 6

The inner man

All young people burn up a lot of energy and we were extremely active. Food was very important to us, and there was always a good deal of speculation what the next meal would be. At breakfast, we tried to wheedle out of the maids what was for lunch; at lunch, what we were getting for tea. A boarder's idea of heaven was cheese, onion and potato pie for Saturday tea, followed by a film in Big School!

I have described the old dining hall and kitchens in Main School. These were converted into the Library in the mid-1950s and the new dining hall and kitchens built in Wykeham garden. I can imagine how relieved the kitchen staff were! In the new hall, we sat on benches at some rather splendid oak tables, set out in five rows across the room, at right-angles to the serving hatches. We sat together in years, with the first years' table nearest to the staff table. Quite wide gaps were left between the foot of each table and the serving hatches and the head of each table and the windows. These allowed free passage, as did the gaps between the rows of tables. A staff table, with chairs, was at the top of the room, at the far end from the entrance doors. At lunch the prefects joined the staff table. At breakfast and tea they sat together at the head of the table nearest to the door.

At breakfast and at tea, the cooked course was placed on the serving hatches in containers. These were collected by the prefects and taken to the head of each table, where there was a serving spoon and pile of plates. Portions were doled out and passed down the table. While for some dishes the portions were already separate, for others, such as the cheese and onion pie, the prefect had to be accurate enough to keep the portions equal and not to run out before he had served the last boy. The technique was to serve small portions and, if any was left, to declare a dividend. Even with something so simple to serve as kippers, there could be ructions: "It's not fair! His kipper is twice the size of mine!"

His kipper is twice the size of mine!

There was no nonsense about cereal *and* cooked breakfast. In the week you got no cereal. That was for Sunday, when it was cornflakes and a boiled egg for breakfast. On Sunday you had a bread roll too. Down the middle of the table were jugs of tea (with milk and sugar already added), plates of school marmalade (breakfast) or school jam (tea) and plates with piles of slices of bread about three-quarters of an inch to an inch thick, spread thinly with margarine and cut across in half. These we called 'slogs'. You had to remain seated throughout the meal, unless getting replenishments from the serving hatch, and so neighbours had to be asked to pass things. Thus you might nudge your neighbour as you were nearing the end of a slice of bread and jam and say: "Slogs, please". He would pass the message on and eventually a plate-full of slogs would start its journey. Quite often it was empty by the time it reached its destination, having been raided *en route*. You then trudged up to get some more. Sometimes, and especially if slogs were being asked for by the junior end of a mixed-year table, there would be the enquiry: "Who for?", when the message arrived. The plate would usually be sent on its way, eventually, but

106

with conditions attached: "Well send it back, then," or: "You'll have to get the next lot".

Lunch was a different routine. The food was, in essence, meat and two veg followed by a pudding. As with the other meals, there was no choice. It was take it, or leave it. The only things on the tables were condiments and jugs of water. You went up table by table to the serving hatch to get your food and the system was a double one so that one set of hatches served one half of the hall and the other the other half. On going up to get your pudding, you took up your dirty plate and cutlery, scraped any left-overs into a special container, put your cutlery in another container and piled up the plates. The cook stood, balefully, near the left-overs tray, daring you to reject her offerings.

It was good nourishing food, and boarders got a pretty well-balanced diet, considering the huge amount of energy we expended. *Cordon bleu* it was not! Among the breakfast dishes were: fried egg on fried bread; bacon and fried bread; tomatoes on toast; beans on toast; sausage and beans; porridge. Lunch menus included: mince, carrots, mashed potato; roast meat, boiled cabbage, boiled potatoes; liver and bacon, canned tomatoes, mashed potato; fish, chips, peas. Puddings might be: jam sponge; spotted dick; stewed fruit; jam or treacle tart; chocolate sponge; rice pudding. Custard was served with all of these, except the rice, and the sponge and the suet puddings were known as 'stodge' and were highly popular. Those on the list I gave were jam stodge, currant stodge and chocolate stodge respectively. For tea there might be: kippers; Welsh rarebit; cheese and onion pie; bangers and mash; baked beans on toast; fish cakes; rissoles.

Sundays brought changes to the weekday menus. Just one cook was on duty, and so cooking was kept to a minimum, with all the preparation and some of the cooking done the previous day. Breakfast was almost invariably: cornflakes, boiled egg, roll and butter, toast and the ubiquitous tea, marmalade and slogs. Lunch: roast meat, roast potatoes, carrots or cabbage, gravy (in jugs on the tables) followed by fruit jelly, milk jelly or trifle with bananas and jam in it. The whole Scragg family joined the staff table at Sunday lunch, where the children, Cathie and Charles, kept the young persons' end of things up by pushing the jelly backwards and forwards between their teeth to their mother's embarrassed annoyance! Tea was spam and salad, a piece of fruit cake, an apple, orange or banana and, of course, tea, slogs and jam. People often used to pocket the breakfast egg for consumption later. As with any institutionally cooked boiled egg, about seventy percent were hard-boiled, twenty-five percent were soft-boiled and five percent were underdone. Bad luck on you if the egg you kidnapped was underdone! If you discovered this at breakfast, you could apply for a replacement. Not so otherwise.

There was one memorable fruit jelly. The boys living in Wykeham had been driven forth on Saturday to pick the crop of red currants in the garden. The maids stripped the fruit from the stalks and these were mixed into a currant jelly for Sunday lunch to liven it up. It did that all right! It was not so much a case of ants in amber, but of a splendid cross-section of the families of the Class Insecta in jelly. There were indeed ants, also bugs, small beetles, flies, aphids, wasps and lacewings, together with some mites and spiders. A scatter of over-looked stalks and leaves completed an artistic arrangement, which these days would have brought the cook recognition alongside such luminaries as Damien Hirst, but then merely drew opprobrium from us. Luckily, this confection was served to the boarders *after* letter-writing, although some of the following Sunday's letters contained graphic descriptions - I know that mine did.

The reason I know this is because it made my mother recall what had happened at Jersey Ladies College in her youth when someone discovered some stray wildlife in the school salad. There had been shrieks and noisy complaints. This behaviour was, according to the Headmistress, unbecoming in young ladies. The correct procedure in future would be to place any livestock quietly aside onto a plate and, without confronting or abusing the kitchen staff, put the plate in the scullery. She would inspect the scullery after each meal and take such action as was appropriate.

Need I say that such a naïve offer was accepted with joy and enthusiasm. The countryside around the College was stripped of the more revolting of its native faunae which were presented in the scullery, tastefully arranged amongst lettuce leaves and on plates, at the next opportunity.

Lunch was a relatively leisurely meal. You collected your food, ate it and left, after Grace had been said. You gained nothing by rushing. Not so in breakfast or tea. Once inspection was over, the duty master said Grace (usually in Latin) and this was the starting gun for an eating race for which Grace at the end of the meal was the finishing tape. Once second Grace had been said, it was a case of 'everybody out', except for the prefects. Since they had lost time at the start by having to serve, this was reasonable enough. The rest hurled themselves onto their benches as soon as first Grace was said and got stuck into the slogs. New boys soon learnt the art of cramming a large tonnage of bread into themselves in the allotted span of twenty minutes. They also learnt the tricks required to ensure no wasteful delays in replacing supplies. You could not ask for more slogs until a plate was empty, and, in the old dining hall, the maids came to you when you held up an empty plate so they could see whether there was still bread on that table. You needed to conceal the last few slogs under the table, on your knees, to ensure an unbroken flow.

Even working at top speed, growing boys could not get all they wanted and so slogs were put with their buttered sides together and were smuggled out in jacket pockets. If a prefect caught you, you lost the slogs, but gained an imposition. If Matron caught you, you lost your head! These ill-gotten gains were usually eaten immediately in corridors or playgrounds. Four was the maximum load - two in each side pocket of the jacket. The pockets were just big enough, but it was quite hard to load up without being seen, because we were packed together pretty tightly on the benches. Having loaded up, there was a distinct risk that your neighbours, in pressing against you, would flatten the slogs, and in the playground it was often a battered specimen that was drawn out from your pocket. Matron's concern was not so much the smuggling of food *per se*, but her knowledge of what boys keep in their pockets and the high probability that a bacterial culture grown from the residues in them, and capable of being impacted into slogs, would be of extreme interest to any pathologist should the worst happen to the eater of these stolen fruits.

Slog smugglers

When I was in Remove, a group of us who were dormitory captains in Coombe Court, collaborated to smuggle slogs on a regular basis. After lights-out, we then collected the electric fire from the Common Room and took it into the tuck-box room in the basement. There it was plugged in, lain on its back and the slogs placed in batches, butter side up, on the protective grill in front of the elements. Being thick, the un-buttered side got well toasted before the margarine oozed through to drop onto the elements. It was surprisingly good, especially if a bit of jam or marmite was available. Although we got rid of the smell pretty well by opening the tuck-box room window, there were still distinct aromas in the entrance hall. We timed our toast sessions for after the duty master's evening round of all the buildings, but Joe Luker lived in the building and had to be neutralised. He was, therefore, invited to join us early on in the venture, and declared that this was Steyning's answer to French toast.

Apart from the three main meals, the only other refreshment provided was a cup of cocoa served in the dining hall between first and second prep and immediately after evening prayers. At this point, the prefects were given one of their main perquisites - prefects' supper. This could be almost anything - cold meat or cheese and slogs; sausages and mash; hard-boiled eggs and slogs. Often there was a slice of cake too. This was eaten, not in the dining hall, but carried in a food container to Main School and eaten in the House Captain's room in the Brotherhood Hall tower. Whatever troubles the day had brought, and whatever reefs lay ahead for the duty prefects in the choppy seas of second prep, you felt, at this point, that God was indeed in his heaven and that all was right with the world.

You could - and did - supplement the official rations. First, you had the contents of your tuck-box. Secondly, you had your pocket money and a further sum banked in the Holland House bank (in my last two years at Steyning I also had my Post Office Savings book with me and could dip into that too if the need arose). Thirdly, you could forage.

Tuck-boxes contained whatever you could persuade your parents to provide. Usually, boys had pots of jam, boxes of 'Swiss' cheeses, pots of meat pastes or other spreads such as peanut butter, syrup, honey, or chocolate spread. These all helped liven up the slogs. Most brought cake - mine were usually a home-made fruit cake and a spiced cake or gingerbread. Biscuits were another 'usual'. Then, inevitably, there were sweets. Because of rationing, most of us were conditioned not to eat very many, but we certainly enjoyed what we could get. Quite a few brought orange squash or some other cordial; one friend always brought a dozen hard-boiled eggs, and most of us had some fruit. Supplies were replenished at half-term, and many letters home contained pathetic accounts of actual or imminent starvation and fervent hopes that a tuck parcel could be put in the post. Great was your joy - and that of your friends - if a tuck parcel actually arrived.

Pocket money could be collected from the House Bank on Wednesday or Saturday mornings after breakfast. The minimum was a shilling, the maximum half-a-crown. The precise amount was decided by your parents. Mine was a shilling, but rose to one-and-six when I reached Remove 1. Although my arithmetic was poor in class, when it came to pocket money my brain shifted up a gear. Long and intense were the debates about best value purchases. Was it better value getting a bar of chocolate costing sixpence, or a quarter of a pound of aniseed balls and a couple of rolls of refreshers for the same price? If you got only the aniseed balls and one roll of refreshers, you would have enough for a seven-penny tin of baked beans. At this point we entered the realm of true economics without knowing it. The tin of baked beans would have to be shared - friends would need to be 'treated', and it was virtually unheard of for anyone to pig the lot themselves. The mental calculation had to be made about what you might get in return. Was a precious spoonful of beans 'worth' a slice of Daisy Day's now rather elderly cake, or a 'dip' of Pop Russell's syrup, or the risk of a promise of reciprocation sometime in the undisclosed future from Tim Medina-Clark? Further, if you 'treated' Penny Craig in the year above you, could he be relied on to protect you from his contemporary, Pat Ballard, who had promised to have your guts for garters after you had accidentally bumped into him in Upper Corridor and made him drop his books. What value did you place on Penny's protection, always assuming you could rely upon it? These and other imponderables occupied a good deal of our time.

Things got even more complicated if there was going to be a film on Saturday. Everyone liked a sweet to suck in the film, but we were realistic enough to know that if pocket money was drawn on Wednesday, neither any money nor any sweets bought with it then would be still with us on Saturday. Many opted for a Saturday withdrawal under these circumstances, but among close friends, pacts were made that if you got your pocket money on Wednesday and spent it in the common good, this would be reciprocated on Saturday.

Having come to such an arrangement you were only halfway there! Next to be decided was what, precisely, would be bought and when - and we are back to the value for money argument, with a shared seven-penny tin of beans on Wednesday traded off against a sixpenny bar of chocolate and a roll of refreshers shared on Saturday. Until

February 1953, when sweet rationing ended, coupons came into the calculation too. There were never enough 'points' to cover a shilling's worth of rationed sweets. You therefore spent your points up to the hilt and then cast around for things such as tiger nuts, crisps, or sub-standard broken pieces of honey-comb toffee to absorb the money.

Among the favourites were the long-lasting gob-stoppers, which changed colour as you sucked your way through the different layers. These were too big, though, to suck surreptitiously in class and had to be spat out into a handkerchief or twist of paper and put in your pocket when the bell went for the end of break. For this reason, aniseed balls were a regular purchase. They were small enough not to be noticed if stuck under your tongue or in your cheek. If they were detected, of course, you had problems: "What are you eating, boy? Spit it out into the waste paper box and see me after the period!"

The boarders also foraged. Most things were fair game and we were certainly willing to try most things. In the autumn there were apples to be 'scrumped' from an orchard at the bottom of the Horseshoe and blackberries in the hedges. We found a sloe bush which had sweeter fruit than most, which made the sloes edible (just!), there were hazel nuts along Spit-handle Lane and pig-nuts could be dug in one or two places. We even tried cutting slices off sugar-beet with our penknives. They were never high on our list and were usually discarded after a few chews. In the summer, the little wild strawberries on the Downs were avidly picked and eaten. At home, I had been shown by a friend how to collect moorhen's eggs. The technique was to find a moorhen building a nest, or one which had just begun to lay. You marked the first two eggs laid, or, if there were eggs in the nest when you found it, all the eggs in the nest. You visited the nest regularly and took one out of every two freshly laid eggs, marking the one you left. This continued until the bird stopped laying. Raw eggs were among the things you could ask the maids to cook for you at tea to supplement your school food and I remember the horror with which Margaret greeted my request for her to boil two moorhen's eggs, gathered as I have described:

"You can't be eating the wee birdie's eggs!"

However, I persisted. Cooked they were and very good they tasted! Then, in 1954, the Protection of Birds Act arrived on the scene and that source of extra food was lost to the legislation.

Scrumping

The farmers also lost a small proportion of crops such as peas, broad beans and wheat to hungry boarders. This was more a case of gathering a few pods or a few ears of wheat and extracting the edible bits as you walked along, rather than any serious and sustained assault. The school gardens also suffered raids on anything that could be eaten raw, with peas and carrots being among the favourites. The Wykeham mulberry was not overlooked, of course, but that was permitted fruit - which took the edge off it!

Finally, there were windfalls, both literal and metaphorical. From time to time, people brought in large boxes of windfall apples. These were placed by the door of the dining hall. We could help ourselves when we went out, and terrible would be the fate of anyone mistreating his apple by playing football with it, or if the cores were used - as they almost always were - as missiles in gang warfare in the playground. The boy who ricocheted a core off Jonah's head as he rounded the end of the physics lab to investigate the noise in the small playground probably did not sit down easily for a week afterwards.

The metaphorical windfall was cake. The duty master at tea had thin, buttered bread, proper jam and a plate of cake. If any of these were left, some of the staff would put them on one of the tables to be shared. The plates were emptied in a micro-second! Arthur Lee went one better. He did not agree with preferential treatment for staff and normally had just a couple of cups of tea and gave us all the food. He rotated this favour around the hall and was very good at remembering who had and who had not, received largesse previously.

I must say that I liked most of the food we were given. The lack of choice was nothing new, there had been no choice at either of the schools I went to previously and there was no choice at home. The only item consistently cooked badly was boiled cabbage, which was always cooked to a slimy and lingering death. For some reason, this was the norm in any institution and in most restaurants then. I have now a friend who lives in Paris and who still tries to avoid coming to stay in England because of our boiled cabbage, sliced white bread and instant coffee! The Steyning Grammar School boiled cabbage of the 1950s is the epitome of what he fears from *la cuisine anglais*!

Chapter 7

Pastimes

For boarders, there were *lacunae* of free time between breakfast and Assembly; in the morning break; in the lunch break; and between the end of school and tea. To this you could add, for dormitory captains and prefects, the gap between lights-out and the time that they had to be in bed. On the half-days of Wednesday and Saturday, there was the pre-lunch shopping hour, the free afternoon until tea and, on Saturday, a free evening. On Sunday, there was a space between church and lunch, and the free afternoon - the Holland House Sunday service occupied the evening.

There was also a short space of time, perhaps half-an-hour, between lights-out and the return of the dormitory captain to go to bed himself. This was, in a sense, stolen free time, because we were not supposed to do anything other than go to sleep. Although someone might occasionally get his bed raided and end up on the floor, together with his mattress and bed-clothes, violent activity was ill-advised since the noise might well attract Authority, with a slipper in its hand. We all had small torches, useful if not essential in the winter, and these were deployed beneath bedclothes to give light for reading. They were also used to light up your face from below to produce 'frightening faces'; put in the mouth and turned on with your cheeks puffed out to give a rather peculiar Chinese lantern effect; or to give the illumination for someone else to make animals or faces with the shadow on the wall of a hand and fingers. I remember in Dormer we took it in turn to whisper to the rest stories we had made up, or plagiarised from books we had read and which the others had not. From what I remember, these would have told a psychologist a great deal about each of us and, in some cases, justified sending for a psychiatrist!

Cheap kits were available too, from which radio crystal sets could be made. These needed aerials, usually a wire concealed along a

116

picture rail or skirting board. Sometimes it was enough to connect the aerial wire to your metal bed-frame. It was possible to pick up Radio Luxembourg with these tiny sets. There was one of these in our dormitory, and it could be heard only by using an earpiece. The owner, however, would give a running commentary on proceedings, especially coming up to a commercial. At this point, the rest of us prepared for action. This needed pencil and paper and someone to hold a torch. Then would come the announcement:

"It's about Austin cars!"

Groans! Everyone stood down!

"Hey! It's dog biscuits! Anybody want a sample?"

A chorus of whispered: "Yeah!"

An address would then be dictated. The following day, those who wanted to sent for the free sample on offer. The dog biscuits, I recall, tasted nicer than the charcoal biscuits that someone got. Various soaps, scents and ointments were sent for by some, but it was things like Marmite, jam, or baked beans that everyone was after and they came along but rarely.

The crystal set gave out news as well as jingles and pop tunes. This would be whispered to us and, quite often, we discussed it until the sounds of the dormitory captain's or duty master's footsteps were heard outside the door. Everything would vanish then - paper, pencils, torches, books, crystal set - and sleep feigned. Fine POW-camp stuff - Colditz could not have improved on it!

We had more scope in officially recognised free time. In Common Rooms, boys read the newspaper or books; made model planes; played games such as five-stones or jacks, marbles, conkers (in their season), chess, table tennis (in Coombe Court); learned new tricks with yo-yos; or told rude jokes. In Dormer, we had a craze for miniature cricket, played with carefully carved bats and little stumps wedged into slots in a small length of wood cadged from Jamie. The ball was usually a marble - which could cause a considerable amount of damage to windows, pictures, light-bulbs or people. On one never-to-be-forgotten occasion someone executing a splendid hook shot managed to hit Drip Walters, the resident master, in what the radio

Miniature cricket in Dormer common room.

commentators usually call 'a painful place' as he came through the Common Room door. Luckily, he took it in good part, remarking merely that Dormer was the only place he knew where you had to wear a cricket box in the Common Room. It was in Dormer too that those coiled metal Slinky toys made their first appearance. These fascinated everybody, staff and boys alike and soon were everywhere. The stairs were in great demand for Slinky races and another challenge was to steer your Slinky 'round the corner' (i.e. across the half-landing) and so get it to walk from the first floor to the ground floor in one go. A snag to all of this was that we were not allowed onto the stairs except to go to the dormitories in the evening or from them in the morning. Hence my alarm when Jonah's hand began cuffing the back of my head and I heard the familiar: "What is this, boy? What is this?", as I watched the first Slinky come down the stairs. Luckily for us all, Jonah was as interested as we were, and even had a go himself before telling us to play with it in the Common Room.

In the playground more active games were played, but there were also restrictions. These were due to the limited space, the proximity of glass in the windows of Main School, and creation of mess. Only tennis balls were allowed, and these were liable to confiscation if they were detected venturing near to a window; conkers was banned in the playground almost annually a couple of weeks into the season because of the litter of broken conkers; paper darts left lying around brought an instant prohibition of these missiles too. Marbles came to an abrupt end once, when a master trod on one lost in Lower Corridor and hurt his ankle.

Among the crazes which swept the playground were balsa-wood gliders. These simple gliders could be set to do aerobatics, like looping-the-loop, or distance gliding. The latter I found more satisfying, but there was a real risk of writing your glider off by having it trodden on accidentally by someone far away from the launching place, or having it rent wing from wing by an irate senior you had struck with it. Aerobatics took place at the top of the playground, away from the trees. Here there were two principal risks. The first was windows. I never saw one actually broken, but it was bad policy to crash your glider on the staff-room windows and Buffer was not very happy when one came in at the open chemistry lab window as he was setting up the apparatus for the first class after break. The second was Johnny's lawn. If a glider went over the high, chain-link fence and onto the Sacred Turf, you were best advised to knock on his study door to ask for permission to retrieve it. To be caught on the lawn without permission guaranteed loss of the glider, if nothing worse, and everyone knew that while you might search the school in vain for the Headmaster when you wanted him, he would instantly appear at your side if you stepped onto the grass.

The same applied to parachutes. For these, you tied four equal lengths of string to a small stone and the other ends of the string to the corners of your handkerchief. The handkerchief was then rolled up carefully round the stone, and the bundle thrown as high as possible into the air. It unrolled, ideally just as the descent began, and formed a parachute which glided back to earth. If a gust of wind caught it as it came down, or if the strings were not of equal length and so the contraption angled its descent the wrong way, Johnny's lawn came into play. While day boys might sacrifice a handkerchief, no boarder could do so. First, your handkerchief had sewn to it a Cash's name tape with your name on it - that is how I came unstuck when my parachute dropped onto the lawn a few feet from Johnny who was walking solemnly across it.   Secondly, if there was no dirty handkerchief in your laundry bag on Monday, Matron would be upon you demanding, with menaces, a dirty handkerchief.   It was not considered a safe defence to point to your parachute hanging high in the conker tree in the playground.   I think it fair to say that the parachute craze did not have Matron's support.

Parachute hung up in a tree.

Particularly when the day boys were not there and the playground was not so crowded, for example on Wednesday or Saturday lunch breaks, or after church on Sunday, the boarders used it for games of tag, usually simple touch tag which took in corridors, the Bog and the fire escape as well as the playground.   There was also chain-he, where you joined the chain when you were caught.   To be caught you had to be touched by one of the two boys at the ends of the chain, but could break through the middle of the chain without being tagged.   The middle of the chain, of course, tried to hold you until one of the ends arrived.   It could get quite violent, and the other risk was that, if the chain was swung round too fast, the end boy left the ground or simply lost control, and was smashed into a wall or a tree.   There was a good deal of technique and strategy involved if it was played seriously.

Even more violent were British bull-dog, played across the top of the playground, and Cock-a-roosha.   In the latter, you all hopped across the playground, arms folded in front of you. The one in the middle, also hopping, tried to barge into someone hard enough to make them put both feet to the ground. If this happened, that person joined the defender in the middle. The numbers of crossers thus diminished, as the number of defenders grew. It was a bit like League rugby without a ball, and played on one leg. To come out unscathed, you had to be able to fall properly, to steer clear of walls, and be able to hop sideways and backwards as well as forward. It was played very hard, but if someone did get hurt - badly winded, seriously grazed knee, bloody nose or split lip - the action stopped and the sufferer ministered to. If we couldn't cope with the damage, the person concerned was escorted by one or two of the others, to see Matron. This, in turn, occasionally meant a visit to the playground by Matron and the strong hint from her that perhaps a gentler game, such as all-in wrestling, might be played instead.

Just about as dangerous were the playground slides which appeared immediately there was a good frost. In the main playground, the slides were to either side. The longer one was against the fence and hedge; the shorter alongside the Chemistry lab and woodwork room, and ending in the protruding bit of the Physics lab wall. It was on this short slide that I spun round after bumping into someone and knocked half a front tooth out - it was replaced with a gold crown which meant that I dazzled people with my smile thereafter. However, the main slide was down the left side of Burdock's Slope. Here we would pour water to give a good sheet of ice and slide down singly or in a chain. Looking back on it, I am surprised that a couple of broken arms were the worst injuries suffered. When things got too hectic; when there was any substantial injury; or when, as happened once, some clown tipped water over the whole of Burdock's Slope, and then even the combined might of the school was unable to get Buffer's car up it, Mr Savage and Mr Nash were sent out with bags of salt. There was then weeping and gnashing of teeth - or if you were like me, gnashing of what remained of your teeth after they had been introduced, forcefully, to the surface of the playground or to the brick gate-post at the bottom of Burdock's Slope.

Slide on Burdock's Slope.

Occasionally, there were fist fights. It was always one-on-one and if one knocked the other down, that was that. It was most unusual that a fight lasted long. The cry of 'Fight!' went up and the normal buzz of playground activity stopped as everyone clustered round and then cries of encouragement started for one or both of the contestants. It was an absolute give-away, and staff and/or School Prefects would be on the scene within minutes. Any of these could bring proceedings to an end immediately and without any thought of being disobeyed or ignored. The only time I remember someone getting expelled was when he leant across in front of the master who had stopped a fight and punched his opponent on the nose. He was isolated in an empty sick-bay immediately and left the school for good the following morning - there were other factors involved in this case, but this reaction following an incident of that kind would have been expected by the boys. A fight meant a visit to your Housemaster or the Headmaster and, if the differences between you and your fellow pugilist remained unresolved, it was not unusual, in the early 1950s, for you to be brought together, without an audience, in a boxing ring in the gym to bring matters to a conclusion. Real fights, as opposed

122

to brief spats or wrestling to establish ascendancy, were pretty rare, especially among the boarders.

After school, hobbies rose in prominence, although the more dedicated boarders indulged in them too in the longer breaks during the day. Some were solitary undertakings which drew no army of followers. Others attracted small groups and spawned societies with a member of staff as official patron. These societies grew up on a wave of enthusiasm, flourished for a while and then faded away as key individuals left the school. The heyday of the Archaeological Society was at the end of the 1940s and it was very active in the early 1950s with the excavation of the barrow on Steyning Round Hill as its focus. The destruction of the barrow and the loss of key seniors like Mansie Manetta saw a downhill slide begin and by 1957 it was all but dead. Tony Marr's enthusiasm saw a Bird Club start up and I remember him trying to teach me the difference between a dunlin and a common sandpiper on a trip to Pagham Harbour. I couldn't even focus the binoculars properly and everything looked the same to me. Tony gave me up as a bad job and, since everyone else seemed to be a bird-watcher, I turned my back on ornithology and concentrated on insects, earning my nickname of Beetle. By the late 1950s, a Natural History Society had been generated and Joe Luker sponsored it. The society had a room at the top of Coombe Court to which members had access any time during the day. There was a display table with an exhibit that changed weekly and involved members being sent forth to collect fungi one week, tree leaves the next, then pond life and so on. There was a microscope; aquaria; vivaria, one of which housed the grass-snake, Houdini, for a short moment in time; and collecting apparatus and identification books which members could use. The advantage of this society was the breadth of the field it covered. Whether it was badgers or fossils that interested you, you were in!

My own passion for insects and other creepy-crawlies landed me in hot water occasionally. A communal puparium of pine processionary caterpillars was dissected to see how many had been parasitised and anyone who was in the room at the time, or shortly afterwards, developed painful rashes from the microscopic hairs drifting up from the dried skins of the caterpillars. Matron's words to me were short and to the point and the room was put out-of-bounds until thoroughly de-loused. She did not approve very much either of the fleas appearing from some old bird nests.

One boy, who had hitherto shown little interest in or aptitude for anything, suddenly found an interest in worms. On the basis of diligent research in text-books and encyclopaedia, a formidable collection of live annelid worms was produced for a Speech Day exhibition. These included the large and active *Nereis*, which surprised someone by biting them! I had myself rewarded all this industry by buying two medicinal leeches from a biological supplier, and these needed feeding. A volunteer was found eventually - we did have the *nous* not to have this as a side-show for parents on Speech Day - and a considerable audience assembled to watch. The victim professed to feeling no pain as the leeches metaphorically tucked napkins into their collars and applied knives and forks to the feast. He was slightly alarmed though when the incisions continued to bleed after the leeches had finished and took himself off to Matron. Once more, Matron came looking for me with a hatchet!

Feeding the leeches

124

In about 1958, we discovered badgers. Ernest Neal's book had been read and inspired us to look for signs on the Downs. There are plenty of signs of course, but our total ignorance of these common animals meant a great deal of detective work involving footprints, claw marks on trees, and identification of hairs and bones before we accepted that the huge holes with their massive spoil mounds and the conspicuous path systems and dung pits at the top of the Rifle Range were indeed the work of badgers. Then, of course, we wanted to see the animals. Their being nocturnal, this raised practical problems.

When I raised the matter with him, Johnny allowed me to go, by myself, on condition that I was back at school at about the time, as I later discovered, that the badgers were coming out! I never did see one while I was at school, but Johnny had enough faith in me to let me roam in the gloaming with all the potential temptations that Steyning could offer around me. After I left, Bunny Whytock, who took over the NHS from me, persuaded Johnny that he should allow selected groups go out at a more realistic time of night and the boys had some good nights of badger-watching. The sett they watched was on Lyons Bank, a couple of miles or more from school and in woods half way up the scarp slope of the Downs. To allow a group of boarders, some relatively young, to go up there at night unaccompanied by staff says a lot about the school and the faith placed in those boys. From all the accounts I received - and believe me I got very full ones - at no time was that faith misplaced.

Johnny used his naturalists and biologists himself from time to time. He was keen on trout-fishing and fished on Wiston Lake. Here he shot a couple of coots and demanded an analysis of their stomach contents - it was all vegetation. His response, when Pop Russell and I asked him why he had shot them, was a classic: "Because they are such nasty, quarrelsome creatures!"

Among the other societies I remember were: a Morris Dance Society, begun by Mr Purver when he arrived in the late 1950s; a Music Society, which listened in the gym to classical records played on the school gramophone; a Chess Club; and a Modelling Club.

The main objective of the Modelling Club was to make model aeroplanes from kits and, having constructed them, to fly them in the Mill Field. They had small petrol engines which turned propellers and were controlled - or not as the case might be - by two wires. The planes thus flew in circles and were launched by someone standing holding the aeroplane at the limit of the wires, starting the engine and throwing the machine into the air once the person at the other end of the wires gave the signal. The theory was that the plane could be brought under control, made to climb and then perform aerobatics. Once the performer got tired of this, or the engine cut out, the aircraft would be brought to earth in a shallow descent to land safely on the

The flying muck-spreader.

grass. That, as I say, was the theory. Need I add that the practice often varied from this ideal. The engine was liable to cut out at any moment, and, were this to happen at a critical point in some complex manoeuvre, disaster loomed large. More often mechanical failure, such as a flap sticking, or over-ambition on the part of the controller, saw aeroplane and earth become as one. This would cause substantial damage and the loss of many hours of patient work with razor blade and balsa wood, paper, glue, dope and paint. The aeroplanes were usually built using detailed plans which came with the kit. Sometimes a novel design was sketched out and tried. Drip Parker built a splendid and sinister machine, which in many respects anticipated the American Stealth Bomber. It was a flying wing which curved back on either side and with the engine mounted in the centre. It was painted black and called The Bat. Alas, its life was short and its maiden flight ended abruptly.

The Mill Field was often shared with cows. These animals, wisely, kept well away while flying was in progress. Traces of their passage often remained and one of the most spectacular high-speed landings was when two very recent cow-pats were scattered to the wide.

The flying expeditions nearly always drew an audience, usually of juniors, all waiting eagerly for a spectacular crash. We were interested in real aeroplanes too. Most of the ones we saw regularly were small bi-planes, such as Tiger Moths, from Shoreham Aerodrome. Monoplanes such as Hurricanes and Spitfires were quite frequent, as was the speedy, double-propellered Wyvern. Meteor and Vampire jets were observed with increasing frequency, and then the very fast Hawker Hunter made windows in the town rattle with the double boom made as pilots broke the sound-barrier off the coast. Vulcan bombers, huge delta-winged machines, made an appearance and in 1957, I think, one coming in low over the sea crashed into houses at Southwick. No-one from the school was among the dead, but the Guy brothers joined the ranks of the boarders while damage to their house was repaired.

Some of the things we did, fall between pastimes and sports and I am putting them here as a bridge between the two.

The first is something I cannot write about with any authority because I was one of the very few who did not join the Scouts. Joe Luker was the Scoutmaster for most of the time I was at the school, although Pog Sauvain was involved with the Senior Scouts later. The scout hut was behind the end of the gym furthest from the physics lab and the gym itself was used for indoor sessions in the weekly meeting held on Thursdays. I cannot remember why I opted out, but I think I decided that the expense of uniforms and other vital equipment, which my family could ill-afford, was not worth it just to learn how to tie knots. My mother had been a Guider in her youth and had already instilled in me far higher standards of camp hygiene, culinary skills, camp layout and so on than the Scouts achieved. As a field naturalist, I was a competent tracker, could identify trees and find wild food, if pressed. One of my chores at home was cutting logs for our fires and I used a lopping axe for preference. By a lucky turn of fate, I had been taught axe maintenance and correct use by a man who had worked as a lumberjack in Canada, and who sent you back to the grindstone if he couldn't sharpen a pencil with your axe - his own standards were higher, he had to be able to shave hair from his arm with his huge felling axe. He also taught me other elements of woodcraft. All that remained seemed to be knots! I must admit, though, that I sometimes felt a bit out of it on Thursdays when I could find no-one to go for a walk with after school and so had to go for a run whether I wanted to or not.

The Scouts went on hikes, camped on the School Field, cooked meals of disgusting appearance under highly insanitary conditions. To hold a Scout camp was to guarantee Matron's appearance in your midst, when you least expected or wanted her to arrive, and with a trenchant attitude, of which Judge Jefferies himself would have been proud, towards unwashed hands or utensils and to food dropped on the ground and then added to the stew.

I may not have been involved with the Scouts, but was certainly involved in Holland House wide-games. *Everyone* was involved in the wide-games - even the walking wounded had parts to play. These were Saturday afternoon or evening affairs and took place at irregular intervals in summer or autumn, but not, as I recall, more than once a term. The House was split into two groups with equal numbers of the different years in each. A flag and flag-pole were issued to each team and a piece of wool tied round everyone's arms. One team set up its base on the Round Hill, the other on Flagstaff Hill on the other side of the Horseshoe. The idea was to capture the enemy's flag and return with it to your base. Both stealth and force were employed and the theory was that once the wool band round someone's arm had been tugged off, that person was dead. That was the theory! In practice everyone battled on 'dead' or 'alive' until any old scores had been settled, everyone was exhausted, or time ran out. Prefects and dormitory captains were particularly vulnerable in all of this, and I remember having some epic wrestling matches with a big, strong lad a couple of years my junior. In one, the pair of us rolled down the very steep-sided 'Knob' on Flagstaff Hill, ending up flat on our backs in a huge bramble bush from which we had to be extricated by a cheering mob of boys from both sides. Traditional opponents, like myself and Graham North, would contrive to meet every time - even if we were on the same side. It was often rough, but never vicious. No-one ever 'won' so far as I know, but the tactics were often well-thought-out and involved decoys and outflanking movements, with people wriggling on their stomachs through the grass or dodging from tree to tree in the woods, looking for enemy sentries, diverting their attention, and then eliminating them. There were too many people moving too quickly to teach us much about real stealth and fieldcraft, but it gave us confidence to move around in the dusk - in the dark in the autumn - and it was fun.

On returning to school there was a roll-call, and Matron and Nurse were available to deal with cuts, grazes, splinters and thorns, if needs be. Once, we found a first-year boy missing and parties were sent with torches to search the ground for corpses. Young Pollock was discovered in a field half way between the Round Hill and Flagstaff Hill. Being rather small, he had felt his best chance of survival, if not of actual success, was to move as inconspicuously as possible from his base towards the enemy's. He had set off crawling, lying flat and motionless, face down, whenever he detected movement. Friend and foe had passed him in the night, but he had got over half way without detection before the search parties, armed with torches, found him. To his relief, I imagine, everyone took it good-humouredly in spite of having had to tramp back to the top of the Downs after a couple of hours of strenuous activity.

Flagstaff Hill, and in particular the stretch from the gate onto the open Down from the track running up the town side of the Rifle Range to the top of the Horseshoe past the Knob, was the focus for most boarders as soon as it snowed. As soon as it was clear that the snow would probably lie for a few days, the announcement was made that we could get the toboggans out. These were home-made, wooden constructions which could carry two if one lay on top of the other - greater loads were often tried but with very limited success and it really was best to go solo. Small consortia were set up, each with a toboggan and, after school, off we would troop, across the Town Field and up Flagstaff Hill. There we took turns in tobogganing down the steepest bit of the track.

An exception to the 'home-made wooden' rule was the Iron Horse. It was five or possibly six feet long, with a wooden slatted seat on a metal frame, mounted on broad metal runners which curled up in the front. It stood about eighteen inches proud of the ground. It really needed a team of reindeer to haul it. This Scandinavian or Canadian migrant was the sole property of Long Dorm. It was virtually impossible to steer and had distinctly homicidal tendencies. It would be hauled to the top of the steepest bit, The Bump. Here grinning seniors, who had seen it all happen before and, indeed, had suffered it in their first year, held it while some half-a-dozen boys stacked themselves aboard, sitting one behind the other. Once all was ready it was given a shove. It usually slid majestically down The Bump, keeping on course for perhaps twenty yards. Then it normally veered right, heading towards a very steep descent to the bottom of the Horseshoe, to reach which would mean passing at tremendous speed through thickets of thorns. However, the grassland at the top of the descent contained many large ant-hills and one of these would bring the expedition to a sudden conclusion by tipping the whole collection of boys off sideways with the Iron Horse upside-down on top of them and flailing its runners in the air. On one momentous occasion it took the anthills as though they were Grand National fences, flinging boys off to left and to right before vanishing into light scrub with one jockey still clinging grimly to it. Luckily he was dismounted too before it hit the thicket through which it pranced before getting delusions of grandeur and disputed the right of way with a tree. As a spectacle it was extraordinary and a scratched cheek was the only injury! Who says that Guardian Angels do not exist?

The Iron Horse rampant.

On another occasion it veered left, making for the precipitous and heavily wooded descent into the Rifle Range. The universal cry of: "Bale out!!" prevented the loss of a quarter of that year's intake.

The 'normal' toboggans you rode on your stomach, and steered with your feet. Even with these, the tyro was likely to find himself confronted with ant-hills and bushes as he wandered, unintentionally, off *piste*, and anyone, however proficient, was likely to come across rider-less toboggans or dismounted riders and would have to take evasive action.

Obviously, we wore layers of sports kit for this activity and the monumental football boots (see next chapter) really came into their own, giving a sure footing (assuming you had not lost all your studs by then) and reliable protection for your feet against all hazards encountered under the snow or protruding from it.

Great fun!

Chapter 8

Sports

We played a lot of organised games on the School Field, half-a-mile away, on the edge of town. One of my earliest recollections was changing into football kit and being shown how to get there. The kit was a school shirt quartered in red and blue, and a white shirt (so that teams could be distinguished readily); pair of shorts which normally came to within four inches of your knee; long football socks into which, if you were lucky, you stuffed shin-pads; and boots. And what boots! They were of stiff leather which covered your ankles. The toe-cap was bulbous and reinforced, and the sole was thick leather into

And what boots!

which were hammered studs. The studs were cylindrical blocks of layers of leather, through which went many steel nails, rather like panel-pins. They stuck out some half-an-inch at their sharp end. These were hammered into the soles of your boots. Three things were likely to happen during the weeks that followed. Studs came out, leaving you lop-sided and the studs scattered like caltrops in the mud of football pitches, ready to puncture any part of you when you fell.

Studs wore down and, instead of presenting a hard but smooth surface to such legs as they contacted, they armed you with talons. As studs wore down even more, the sharp ends of the fixing pins were driven through the sole and into you. In consequence, most boys lined their boots with thick cardboard. These lethal weapons were secured to you by several fathoms of boot-lace which you wrapped around instep and ankle. To complete the ensemble, we had thick woolly sweaters to keep us reasonably warm on the trek to and from the field.

That first time, we clattered out into Church Street under the guidance of Spud Crannigan, round by Chantry Green - and the pavement on that corner is the same collection of small blocks of different stones I remember so vividly from that first excursion (another of these precious small landmarks!) - round the back of the houses in Highland Croft, down the slope, across Tanyard Lane and along a twitten to a plank bridge over the stream. Up past the town football field (then just an open field), along the track between the Secondary Modern School, its playing fields and the houses of the Shooting Field estate and in through a stile to our playing field. The pavilion - a Nissan-hut, with the groundsman's store, his shelter, a toilet and a changing room and showers, used by day boys and visiting teams - was by this entrance.

A hedge separated our field from the Sec Mod's. About twenty yards in from the hedge were two small clumps of trees and along the far side of the field ran a belt of trees. Assorted football pitches were scattered about in likely places. The cricket square was pretty central, but more towards the pavilion than the main road side. The hockey pitch, running track and associated pits and circles for athletics, migrated from place to place during my years at the school.

That, basically, was that. What we lacked in terms of facilities we made up for in enthusiasm. You needed enthusiasm, might I say, to enjoy football with those colossal boots; yours rooting you to the spot and everyone else's, friend and foe, clattering into you at the slightest movement of the ball in your direction. The ball was the only thing on the pitch a match for those boots. It was leather, with a rubber air-bag inside, which was inflated, using a hand or foot pump, through a valve. The valve was then tucked, with difficulty, into the casing and the slit in the case closed with a leather lace, using a metal lacing needle on a wooden handle. Even dry, those balls were pretty heavy. When wet they got a lot heavier. Heading a wet ball coming at any speed was ill-advised. It really could knock you out, and if the lace caught you, it would cut you into the bargain. I only saw the ball thoroughly beaten once. It was in a staff match and Drip Walters, a rugger player, was in goal for the staff. He gave one goal kick such a toe-poke that the ball burst, ascending to an enormous height, making extremely vulgar noises as it rose, and coming down in a soggy heap on the half-way line with an air of total disillusionment.

Others were skilful at football; I was not. I could kick the ball quite hard, though inaccurately. This meant I could also kick people quite hard and so my undistinguished career as a soccer player was carried through at full back. Since I was left footed, I was made left back in most of the teams, formal and informal, that I played in. My technique was simple and worthy of the Wimbledon Crazy Gang. On getting the ball and approaching an opponent, I would toe-punt the thing at him as hard as I could. If it missed, it sailed up-field into the realms of the proper footballers in my side. If it hit him, I had another go at the rebound and we laid the corpse on the touchline. My own most painful memory is of a House match in which Holland seniors were playing Cuthman, I think. At any rate, on the opposing side was the School First XI centre forward, the large and robust Bert Burstow. He was right-footed and I, as I say, was left footed. We had a fifty-fifty ball spinning near the edge of the Holland penalty area and we both had some fifteen or twenty yards to go to reach it. We arrived, flat out and head on, kicking the ball simultaneously. Had we both been left footed or both been right footed, all would have been well. As it was we met bosom to bosom with a crack that could be heard all round the field. The ball, I was told, went straight up into the air. Shocker, who was refereeing, was amazed that both of us were not only still alive, but were basically unharmed. Stunned for a moment and a bit winded, but that was all.

Day boys and boarders used the field for Form Games which we had class by class once a fortnight. The last two periods of the afternoon concerned were cancelled and the masters teaching those periods were referees or umpires for the session. Bitter was the disappointment if heavy rain or some other meteorological catastrophe led to a message being sent in by Mr Hawes, the groundsman, that Form Games were cancelled. Form Games was our one chance to play with and against day boys who were our contemporaries. It also gave people a chance to assess ability and short-list people for the school teams.

For boarders, there were House Games, often once a week, but usually once a fortnight, when all the boys trooped up to the field on a Wednesday or a Saturday afternoon to knock bits off each other. For many, this was totally insufficient and most afternoons saw groups dashing off after school to beg a pitch for a game, or, if this were not possible, to mark out a pitch for a kick-about on some spare ground. The same applied to hockey, cricket and athletics in their seasons. In the Christmas and Easter terms, there was also cross-country running. With very few exceptions, all boarders did some cross-country and indeed you had to have a cast-iron excuse to avoid entering the School Steeplechase. This annual event was a handicap race (by age, not by ability!) with five minutes between the first year and the Upper VI, over courses which were between four and five miles long. One year, the course went across the Town Field and the Mill Field, up the cart-track in a testing climb to the barn, down to and through Wiston Springs, across a field in which you contested rights of passage with a rather frisky horse (removed for the actual day, but an ever-present hazard during practice), past Wiston House, across the Park and round the back of Wiston Lake, over the fields to Charlton Court Farm and back across the Mill Field. The race began at the junction of Church Street and The Twitten and the finishing line was the gates into Coombe Court. The final sprint down The Twitten was often an exciting one.

Another course brought into play stretches of the Steyning to Partridge Green road and later (on a double bend!) the main A283.

Even with far less traffic then than now, these bits provided some anxious moments for the staff directing simultaneously traffic and some two-hundred and fifty boys travelling roughly at right-angles to it. By the time we had reached the A283 the field had run two and a half miles, some over heavy mud around Wappingthorn, and was well spread out. On that particular course, we met a gate in the old deer-park which was around eight feet high. Being a serious cross-country runner, I put in practice on that gate so that you hit it at speed about four feet up, flipped over in a gate-vault and were off running immediately. I also instructed other boarders in this art. One of my disciples reported that he had booted another competitor in the face in the process and had knocked him off, if not out. However, as he said: "It was only a day bug!" So that was OK!

It was only a day-bug.

The steeplechase was an 'all join in' event, with serious runners competing among themselves and the rest having less intense competition, or none at all. I once overheard a panted question as I cut my way past stragglers: "Have you got the matches?" and hardly think that that group of athletes had finishing in the top thirty as their target.

Although the handicap of five minutes doesn't sound a lot I can assure you that it is. Some of the juniors were excellent runners and when a fair-to-moderate runner like me had to give a couple of minutes to a future Olympic athlete in the shape of Chris Carter, who could beat me round the course without the two minute bonus anyway, you begin to see the challenge. The best I ever did was sixth, when I was in the middle school and old enough to pulverise those younger than me and, simultaneously, have maximum advantage over those older than me thanks to the handicap!

A lot of us ran for fun, or trained for the House and School teams. We would run along the tracks going up onto the Downs, tracks which get me out of breath to walk up now! I also remember running from Steyning to Sompting, along to Shoreham and back past Beeding Cement Works, through Upper Beeding and Bramber to Steyning. For fun!!

In my last two years I trained the Holland House junior team and tried to bring in a bit of variety. I had read about a Swedish system in which you used things lying about the landscape as 'apparatus'. You ran until reaching, for example, a small tree trunk, and used it for lifting exercises before running to the next possible instrument of torture, and so on. I plotted a course taking us - at an easy jog or even a brisk walk over the steepest sections - up the cart-track onto the top of the Downs. Near the top was a beech tree with a sturdy branch at right-angles to the trunk and about five or six feet above the ground. When I had tried the course myself I had found that to do even a couple of pull-ups was difficult after an uphill mile of running. Therefore, I confronted the team with this branch and ordered at least one pull-up from each. As the mob hung gibbering from it, I noticed the smallest, a boy called Kopecek who had just squeezed into the squad, standing contemplating both branch and his colleagues with an air of polite interest. I invited him to join them: "You too, Kopecek!"

"What, me?!"

"Yes, you!"

"Will this do?", as he swung up to do a hand-stand press-up on top of the branch!

Well, if you forget you have the best junior gymnast in the school beside you, you deserve the cheeky, but friendly, grin I got when I called him a clot and told him to come down.

We hurled large flints about in a field on top of the Downs; swung, using first one arm and then the other, from tree to tree in a precipitous descent through a thicket of young ash trees to Wiston Springs; splashed through an arm of the pool; and began to trot down Mouse Lane. At this point, on a level and hard surface, someone hurt his knee and I got some extra weight-training myself carrying him back to school.

After that, we had the bright idea of a hare-and-hounds. The idea of using torn-up paper to mark the trail was discarded on the basis that Johnny might join the field armed with a cane if he found boys littering the town and surrounding countryside on quite that scale. Jamie couldn't - or wouldn't - supply us with saw-dust. Eventually we decided to use blackboard chalk to chalk directional arrows at all junctions. The hares were to be me, as the fastest, and Kopecek, as the slowest. We were given five minutes start and headed down Kings Barn Lane towards the river, Kopie going the direct route and me taking diversions - which deceived no-one.

Leaving the lane, we crossed the fields to the Iron Bridge over the Adur, followed the path to Beeding Church and went back to school through Bramber and Castle Lane, again with me making detours. We will never know whether or not any of these would have deceived the hounds. About fifteen minutes after we had arrived back, we thought we had better try to find the others. I had dreadful thoughts about someone being swept down the Adur on the falling tide, so we trotted back to the Iron Bridge. Kopie stood on top of the arch and eventually saw the rabble trailing across the flood-plain to the north. Our trail

Kopie spied them to the north.

had been to the south and the arrows were still clearly visible on the bridge to prove it.

They had been too clever by half! They knew we were trying to out-wit them and when they saw, as they said, arrows indicating south, but two white running vests in the distance to the north, they took it that we had swung north, having taken a south diversion, and headed for the vests rather than following the arrows. After ten minutes or so of wet and muddy adventures with drainage dykes, they found themselves confronted by a couple of irate swans which, with hissing and wing flapping, drove them further north. They were just returning from this, when they saw us on the bridge.

After that, it was back to running round the Horseshoe!

With a few exceptions, day boys did not play games to this extent. Most boarders were very fit and Holland House won most of the games trophies on offer. In athletics and cross-country, it was a disaster of the first magnitude if Holland did not win at junior, intermediate, and senior levels. When it came to totting up athletics 'standards', Holland was usually out of sight of the other Houses.

Standards, as the name suggests, were times or distances for the different events which showed a reasonable standard of proficiency for the different age-groups. You could go up to the School Field any evening after school over a specified period of time in the summer term to try for standards in as many events as you could. Some were easier than others, most were challenging, but not too challenging. Staff were on hand with stop-watches, tape measures and lists on which to record successes. The events on offer were: 100 yards; 220 yards; 440 yards; 880 yards (intermediates and seniors only); 1 mile (intermediates and seniors only); 100 yards hurdles; high jump; long jump; triple jump; pole vault; shot; discus; javelin.

A House list was prepared showing names on one axis and events on another. Prefects kept a close check on who had got what and frequently Holland House had the three-line whip sent out: "Everybody will go up to the Field today!"

Some of our athletes were very good indeed. Chris Potter with a hundred and eighty feet in the senior javelin; Rob Smith with 9.9 seconds for the 100 yards; Chris Carter in the 880 yards before going to the Tokyo Olympics in the 800 metres. Proficiency in one particular event led to an amusing situation when a scratch school team competed in a triangular match with Steyning A.C. and a team from Brighton. The event took place on the Town Field. The sand-pit for the long jump was a small one. This caused no problems with the long jump since the board was set well back. In the warm-up for the triple jump, however, the two competitors from the school, Mousey Capelin and Birdie Raven, sought me out as Athletics Captain to resolve a problem. They were getting to the edge of the pit with the 'step' element of the jump and would clear the pit completely with the 'jump' element. Fine, said the organisers, let's set the board back. Once this was tried none of the other competitors could get into the pit at all. While Mousey and Birdie were in the middle forties, the rest were landing at least ten feet short of them. Eventually it was agreed that two boards would have to be used; one for the school and one for the rest. The boot was on the other foot in the javelin. One of the Brighton throwers was an over two-hundred foot thrower and could out-throw me with a run-up of a couple of paces. He was unhappy that the judges were too close to him. They ignored him so he threw one just level with them. They retreated behind a cricket scorers' hut for his next effort - which he put through the roof of the hut. They got the message!

As Athletics Captain in my final year, it was the pole vault which caused me most problems. We used an inflexible aluminium pole and the landing pit was sawdust. While experts such as Chris Bachelor managed with no problems, less proficient pole-vaulters broke arms, sprained ankles and wrists and damaged backs and knees to the extent that I had to ban anyone in the School Team, other than the pole-vaulters, from having a go. Had I not, there would have been few of the team left intact!

The throwing events were potentially lethal, especially when half the school was milling about all over the field attempting 'standards'. No-one was ever badly damaged, although one shot-putter only escaped by inches when the shot slipped in his hand and went straight up instead of forwards. A badly directed discus was the most likely missile to score a hit since these skidded off the grass and a few legs were bruised in this way. Those waiting to have their turn with the discus had to stand behind the thrower, and many preferred to get behind a tree as well when following an enthusiastic, but inexpert, thrower. Javelins could also bounce, especially on wet grass, if they came down flat instead of point first. One of my throws did just that and had a group of boys scattering and jumping as the javelin hissed through their midst in a cloud of spray like a black mamba on the war-path.

My own greatest ignomy was reserved for the 100 yards hurdles. The hurdles were wooden and the wood or bamboo bar was capable of being set at three heights for junior, intermediate and senior races. Whilst not very good at hurdles, I found the senior 'standard' within my compass and was confident enough as I lined up in an attempt to cross this relatively easy one off my list. Shocker (it would be!) was the starter and we all got away with no problem. My mind must have been elsewhere, because I found myself suddenly confronted with the first hurdle and with absolutely no idea what I was supposed to do next. In the event, I treated it as I would have done the edge of a swimming pool; rose more or less gracefully over it head first, landed on my hands and, finding the grass less yielding than water, executed a neat forward roll, ending up on my feet confronting hurdle number two. By this time most of my fellow competitors had finished, leaving the School Athletics Captain alone with his PE master, who, when he eventually stopped laughing, remarked that my technique was certainly novel, but he did not think that it would win many races and recommended a return to more orthodox ways. For the rest of the afternoon he began laughing again and shaking his head whenever he caught my eye.

A new technique for hurdling?

Swimming was not an official sport but a leisure activity in the summer for boarders who made up the groups taken on Wednesday afternoons by Digger to the King Alfred Baths in Hove. We travelled on the Steyning Stinker to Hove station and walked from there to the baths. It was here that I learnt to swim and to dive off the side and off the spring-board - the high boards were too much for me and I never even jumped off them!

When I first arrived at the school, boxing was very much an official sport and no-one in Holland House escaped. In fact, on the first Saturday evening of my first term, all the boarders went to the gym, were armed with gloves like young pillows and, having been paired up, were put into make-shift boxing rings to do their worst to one-another. I cannot say that I enjoyed this at all. I subsequently managed to evade the inter-House matches and contrived, without much difficulty, to lose my first fight in the appropriately named School Knockout which eventually left a Junior, an Intermediate and a Senior Champion. Because he was a class above anyone else, Chris Potter was not allowed to enter. To the regret of many of his opponents, Chris's brother Micky *was* allowed to enter and his fights rarely lasted long. When Chris left, the boxing wound down and was dead by the mid-1950s.

Even before being blooded in boxing, I had taken part in the Holland House new boys' run. The better runners in the second year were included and were asked to guide us round the bottom of the Horseshoe and see if any of us were good at cross-country. A prefect brought up the rear and other luminaries of the House cross-country squads arranged themselves near the finish or on Town Field to pass critical - and often loudly vocal - judgement on our efforts. One second-year, running just in front of me, looked a bit weedy and knock-kneed and I stuck to him, thinking that once I got near enough to home to know where the hell I was supposed to be going, I could pass him. How misleading appearances can be! Drip Parker was a pretty good and very keen runner. He was also a ruthless one and finding me closer to him than he liked half way round, managed to slam a gate on me just as I arrived at it, thinking (fool!) that he was going to hold it open for me! Although Drip finished well ahead of me, I had done enough to be noticed as a possible future recruit to the junior squad.

A year or two ago I found the remains of that little gate, now replaced by a squeeze-gate, lying rotting behind a new fence. The metal catch in which Drip had so nearly jammed my fingers that September afternoon in 1951 was there, though. Another small landmark!

Old gate rotting away.

Chapter 9

O, who will o'er the Downs so free?

After lunch, all the boarders, except for the VI Form, went to Big School for Names. The duty prefect read down the House list and people said what they were going to do between the end of school and tea-time. The VI Form wrote their arrangements on a piece of paper and handed this to the prefect after lunch. This ceremony had a serious purpose - if someone was missing at the tea-time roll-call, at least people knew where to start searching for them. If you were going on a run you just said 'run' which rather defeated the purpose, but the prefect might ask where you intended to go. For organised games, you said 'Field' or 'Swimming'. If you were not involved in sport, Scouts, detention or anything of that sort, you went out for a walk. Until you reached the VI Form, you had to go out in pairs or threes. More than three was a gang and not allowed, but once away from the town, groups often joined up by chance, or by design.

Talking on the Knob.

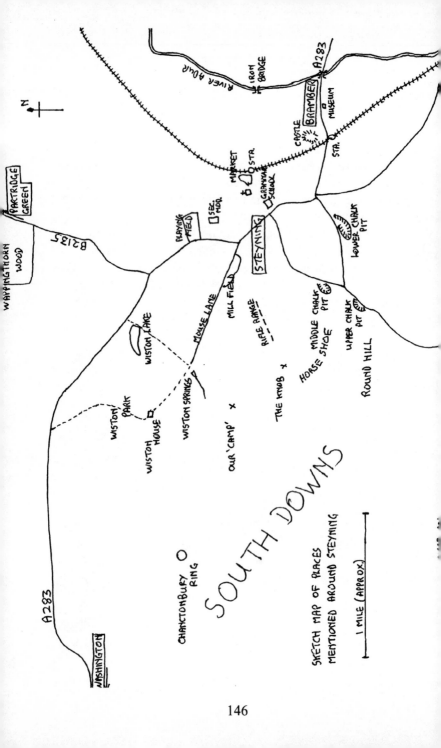

SKETCH MAP OF PLACES MENTIONED AROUND STEYNING

1 MILE (APPROX.)

There was often a good deal of negotiation during and after lunch. The opening question was: "Are you going out with anyone?". If the answer was no, this led to: "Can I come out with you?" and if you agreed, the questioner followed up by asking where you suggested going. You had done him a favour by giving him a partner and so you had the choice. If a third boy then asked one or other of you whether you were free, you responded that you were, for example, going up Mouse Lane with McNiff. Finding you had a pair and not a threesome, the boy might ask to come too, and both of you had to agree. If a fourth now bobbed up, you had a cast-iron reason for rejecting him out of hand if you wanted to, or if he was one of the gang, your threesome absorbed him by dividing again and making up two pairs. Should all negotiations fail, you said, miserably: "No arrangements," when your name was called out. The prefect would tell you to see him after Names. This was the signal for frantic miming across Big School, trying to negotiate to join a pair you heard giving in their names, or from a couple of friends taking pity on you, or from another singleton. It was rare to go for walks with anyone not in your year and, although a prefect might compel two singletons from the same year to join up, he was very unlikely to try it on people from different years, and most prefects did not force people who disliked each other to go out together - it was just asking for trouble.

Names had its own vocabulary which, while perfectly intelligible to us, sounded odd to anyone else. "Are you going out with anybody?" is bad enough. To it though you can add a boy going up to the duty prefect just before he began the roll-call to ask: "Can I make arrangements?", meaning that he wanted to move about to conduct whispered negotiations as the list was being read. Then, the prefect might find someone rushing up at the end to ask: "Can I change my name?", meaning that he wished to amend his arrangements in some way. Anyone staying in school had to have permission from a member of staff, usually Matron if you were unwell, hurt or just out of sick-bay. If you simply said: "Staying in," the prefect invariably asked whose permission you had and so, if it was Matron, you said "Staying in with Matron" when your name was called.

Walks were of two kinds. On full school days, there was less than two hours between the end of school and tea. Time had to be left to clean yourself up before tea, and it took a few minutes to get ready to go out once the last bell went at twenty to four. You were looking at an hour and a half maximum, realistically. On the four full days, walks were short. On Wednesday, Saturday and Sunday you had three to four hours to play with, and so could go further, or indulge in activities which took time.

New boys were taken in a gang on walks by prefects so that they got to know the immediate locality and got some idea what was on offer. In the first week that I was there, we were taken up to the Round Hill for our first walk. The next was round the bottom of the Horseshoe - which we had been made to run round by then. We were also shown how to get to the Iron Bridge across the Adur. On Sundays, for the first few weeks, we went on longer new boys' walks - up to Chanctonbury Ring, for example. On one never-to-be-forgotten Sunday, Chris Potter marched our eleven-year-old legs the six miles or so to Partridge Green, left us standing for a while as he vanished - probably to have a chat and a cup of tea with a girl-friend, we reckoned - and then marched us back. Unfortunately, we could not match the pace he had envisaged. Another prefect cycling by was asked to give the smallest of us, Peter Puttock, a cross-bar back to school and to warn Jonah that we were going to be late for tea. We got back just after tea had finished, with our legs worn down to stumps and very anxious about our food. We need not have worried! Jonah had ensured that our table was not raided and had prevailed on the kitchen to find us something extra. Although he came to talk to us to make sure we were in one piece and to instruct anyone with blisters to see Matron, I did notice him speaking also to Chris Potter. I imagine that time/distance calculations were involved in their conversation and the reasonableness, or otherwise, of expecting eleven-year-olds to keep up a steady four to five miles per hour for three hours!

These walks did help us to find our way around, and there was on Big School wall a framed two-and-a-half inch to the mile Ordnance Survey map, showing the area for about ten miles around Steyning. This was helpful in plotting our mischief and got us familiar with names of places and with map-reading. Although we roamed on foot occasionally up to five or six miles from school, our real territory was quite small. There were within it, honey-pot areas or specific places to which we gravitated.

For short walks, three routes stick in my mind.

Hugely popular in the Christmas and Easter terms with the first two years, was Mouse Lane. The springs welling up in it below Charlton Court Farm gave rise to a small winter-bourne, known by us as 'The Musselaney'. It had small pools and rapids in it, and from a point some thirty yards below the springs it was navigable by stick 'boats' which we raced against each other to the point where it went into a culvert under the main road. There were elaborate rules about when you might and when you might not assist your craft. Weird and wonderful were some of the boats constructed at school and brought to compete. Most were completely unseaworthy and were soon discarded for the straight, six to twelve inch, pointed lengths of hazel or elder used more normally. Mike McNiff managed to perpetrate the ultimate in bad design, *HMS Spikey*. It was about nine inches long and made of 1½" x ½" deal, with upperworks into which

Boat-racing in Mouse Lane.

149

were hammered an inordinate number of different sized nails to simulate guns. The *Tirpitz* paled to insignificance alongside the might of the armament. However, there was no way that it could be made to float other than upside down. It then snagged every one of the main obstructions it encountered in the deeper sections and would not go down rapids at all. Our team of nautical experts concluded that it was clearly an anti-submarine vessel, since its armament was permanently underwater, and the owner and designer consigned it to the culvert, where it probably remains to this day.

Apart from boat-racing, we could walk up to Charlton Court and into the top of the Mill Field. Here model aeroplanes might be flying to provide spectacle, and we often walked back across the drive outside Court Mill, whose owners were happy to let us do so and look at the trout in the outfall stream and, with permission, to stand on the dam to look across the mill-pond.

A second favourite short walk was up Newham Lane. At the foot of the Downs you had a choice. You could continue up the lane, or divert right onto the lower slopes of the Round Hill and into the east part of the Horseshoe. Although this is now mostly ash woodland, in the early 1950s it was mostly grassland and grazed by cattle. Just inside the gate into the field was a large, circular, concrete horse-

Horse-trough at the foot of the Round Hill.

trough. As well as providing for the cattle, this was a superb open air aquarium with clear water, pond weed and a rich pond-life. We often brought jam jars and fished for specimens to take back. It was beside this trough that we once found a dead grass-snake four feet long, which we carried back in triumph to present to Joe Luker for pickling in formalin. Further up the field was a thick hedge (still there now) and this was a favourite assembly spot for second year boys on the look-out for first-years to ambush. You risked losing your shorts if you approached the hedge incautiously!

If, on the other hand, you went on up the lane, you had the choice of two chalk-pits. The first, known as Middle Chalkpit held a corrugated iron barn in which the dust-carts were kept. If the men were around, we kept away - they chased us off if they saw us. If the barn was occupied, all we might do was throw chalk onto the roof from the top in order to improve our vocabulary. The men knew words we had not heard before. If no-one was there, we would go in. A favourite game was throwing lumps of chalk at bits of the cliff which looked loose to try to make 'avalanches'. We would scramble up too and quarry away to de-stabilise larger chunks and create more impressive 'avalanches'. Any good fossils or pieces of iron pyrites we found in the process would be stuffed into pockets and taken back with us.

The second chalk-pit, the Upper Chalkpit, is at the side of the road across to Sompting, above its junction with Newham Lane. One section contained old petrol/oil storage tanks sunk into the ground and half-full of water - this bit is now a small nature reserve. The other section is a steep slope of bare chalk and we would scramble to the top, minding out for adders, and slide down the chalk. Small wonder we often had trouble polishing shoes and brushing mud off trousers and our navy-blue macs!

If, instead of going up the Bostal Road to the Upper Chalkpit, you turned left to go down it back towards Steyning, you came, after a few minutes, to the Lower Chalk Pit - now a housing development called Mount Park. This was bigger than the other two and had the remains of old kilns and other buildings in it. It seemed a popular place for boys older than we were, and I didn't go there often. I believe that it was a place we were supposed not to go, but it was popular among the intermediates.

The whole walk 'round the roads' was about a mile and a half and it also was a favourite training run for juniors, being a mile less than the bottom of the Horseshoe, which was their course for inter-House cross-country.

The third of the popular short walks was to Bramber, which was reached along the main road, or diverting south along Maudlin Lane, or by going along Castle Lane, crossing the railway at an un-manned crossing. In Bramber there were two main objectives; the castle and the museum.

At the castle we explored the ruins, lying on our backs under the remaining wall of the keep which, if the clouds were moving over it, you would swear was falling onto you, or clambering on the walls to pretend that we were sentries. The steep slope into the moat was perfect for sliding down on your heels, or for rolling stones down upon your friends (and enemies) as they walked along the bottom. Wild clematis, Tarzan's Creeper, grew up many of the trees and on some strands you could swing out high above the moat. We split into small gangs to storm and to defend different parts of the castle and knocked bits off ourselves as well as, I regret to say, the ruins. The amount of mud you accumulated was only marginally less than that gained from playing in the chalk pits!

Bramber Museum was like a small brick and flint-built barn, whose principal exhibits were animal tableaux created in the previous century by the local, self-taught taxidermist, Walter Potter. These included among many others 'The Kittens' Wedding'; 'The Burial of Cock Robin'; 'The Rabbits' Village School'; and 'The Guinea Pigs' Cricket Match'. Above, below and around these were layer upon layer of exhibits. Like a snow-ball rolling down a hill, once started it grew of its own volition, accreting items as time went by. These ranged from some fine and valuable authentic face masks from the Cameroons, and rare feathered ornaments from Brazil, to oddities from local farms - duckling with four legs; kitten with two faces;

Swinging on Tarzan's Creeper.

153

piglet with three legs - and a piece of granite from Cecil Rhodes' grave! There were cats found mummified in a local chimney, stuffed birds, wasps nests, minerals, fossils, assorted weapons and ornaments from far and wide, butterflies, beetles, musical instruments, a baked apple one hundred years old, models, game trophies, finds from Bramber castle, bits of old ships, old bank notes and coins including a silver penny minted in Steyning during the reign of Edward the Confessor, a twelve-foot cabbage stalk from Jersey, a man-trap, walking sticks, jockeys' scales, and, unforgettably, a donkey's jawbone because, as the guide book remarked, Samson slew the Philistines with the jawbone of an ass. Although the curator, Eddie Collins, Walter Potter's grandson, had tried to introduce a semblance of order, the constant trickle of new items and the totally random nature of the assemblage made this impossible to maintain. Amongst the logical sequences and groupings, glorious chaos reigned from floor, where one exhibit, a stuffed Jack Russell called Spot, had to have its face washed regularly to remove the ice-cream which young children had 'shared' with it, to the roof and beams from which exhibits such as stuffed albatrosses were suspended. Glass cases housing the animal tableaux and the other exhibits ran at several levels around the walls and down the centre of the room. The exciting jumble is illustrated by the following extract from the guide-book: "210. Head of Tiger. 211. Cannon ball, grape shot, spurs, keys and pottery found in the Bramber Castle grounds. 212. Parts of Antlers, Bison's skull and horns, the remains of four Elephants' tusks and various bones found at Beeding Garage when installing petrol storage tanks in 1925. 213. Scorpions, Locusts, Centipedes etc from Central Africa. 214. Tin hat painted with flags, crests, names etc. 215. Sole of Elephant's foot. 216. Woodcock."

Eddie would not usually charge us an admission fee, especially since we never had much time to spare before we had to leave to go back to school. He also knew very well that we would bring our parents and siblings to see the museum, and could charge them. It was said by us that you would always see something you had not noticed in previous visits, no matter how many times you went there. I think that this was true. My own particular delight was a musical box which, if you put a penny into the slot, would play one or two of its considerable repertoire. The tinkling notes made as the drum with its little metal pegs revolved, is a vivid memory. It seemed magical then.

The museum was known far and wide. Eddie and his wife Nell got great pleasure meeting visitors from all over the world - although Eddie said he was a bit taken aback when he looked at the card given him by a quiet and unobtrusive American, who had chatted to him about the exhibits, to find he had just spent half-an-hour with Walt Disney! I became good friends with Eddie and Nell, staying with them after I had left school and helping re-arrange things, making scientific apparatus for my studies and taking and processing photographs for reports. They had a fund of stories about the area, its residents and the museum and we spent a lot of time helpless with laughter. Eddie was an Old Boy of the Grammar School, but had not enjoyed his time there, which must have been in the late 1920s or early 1930s. The difference between the school when he went to it and the school when I was there was not much less than the difference between it as it is now and as it was in the 1950s. I was unable to get him to visit the place again, except when he came to see me briefly after I hurt myself quite badly in 1958 and was in sick-bay. He was the last in the direct line of descent from Walter Potter and when he died in 1970, Nell couldn't keep it going by herself, the museum closed and its exhibits were dispersed or destroyed. What a pity! It was a remarkable, unforgettable and stimulating place - an Aladdin's Cave of riches to imaginative and inquisitive boys.

On half days and Sundays we were expected to go further. For example, if you gave your name in as 'Mouse Lane' you would be told to go to Wiston Park or Wiston Lake, which took you a couple of miles further.

Wiston Park was not especially popular, except at the end of the Christmas term when we had permission from the owner, John Goring, to collect mistletoe with which to decorate the buildings and then to take home with us. I confess now to a totally unintended crime! Walking across the Park with Dai Tas (I think), we were

155

caught in a rain squall and took shelter in a hollow oak. Cobwebs festooned the space and, passing the time, I got out the matches for lighting camp fires I was carrying (against school rules) and struck one to see whether the cobwebs would burn. The net result was a smouldering patch on the dry rotted wood. The more we scraped at it to put it out the more the sparks flew to ignite further patches. It got eventually far beyond our capacity to control and we fled into the storm to put distance between us and the tree. Looking back from quarter of a mile away, smoke was clearly visible and when I saw the spot a few months later, only a charred stump remained.

Wiston Lake was a popular spot and we played round the margins and climbed trees. In the winter, we skimmed stones or pieces of ice across the frozen surface and, if the ice was thick, would tentatively venture onto it, retreating rapidly at the first echoing, pinging 'Craaack'. Going onto the ice was not encouraged by Authority, nor was playing on the fisherman's punts, chained to trees, near a locked hut in which oars and other items were kept. Since one of the fishermen was Johnny, you were never sure when he was likely to appear and this led us to exercise more restraint than we would have shown otherwise. Johnny was quite likely too to commandeer any boys in the vicinity to bale or clean punts and to generally make themselves useful in ways pleasing to him, but not so pleasing to us. From time to time, a work-force was recruited from VI Form boarders to take the punts out to drag excess pond weed from the lake - an exhausting and dirty game!

A track joined the top of Mouse Lane to the main road and ran from just inside the Park to the Lake, across the dam and up to the main road. Further fishing lakes now exist where the track ran. A short way down the track from Round Robin Lodge was a tied cottage in which lived a gentleman of ferocious mien, who wore a fringe beard and was known to us as 'Hairy'. Just across a narrow field from Hairy's house was a small sluice in the stream leading from Wiston Springs. This we would dam to flood the field, if the coast was clear. Once we did this when the coast wasn't clear and had to run for our lives from a rapidly moving and *molto furioso* Hairy.

Wiston Springs was a small pool formed by throwing a concrete dam across a small valley down which a stream flowed from springs at the foot of the Downs. The dam had cracked and the water reached the top only after heavy rain - although we did our best to plug the leaks. This spot, secluded amongst trees, was a magnet for the first three years. We used logs up to six feet long and four or five inches thick to play 'torpedoes' off the dam, angling our shots so as to be able to retrieve our torpedo from one of the banks. Since all the floating logs eventually drifted to the dam we always had ammunition when we arrived. We climbed trees, 'smoked' small, dry bits of Tarzan's Creeper and explored. A dead fox yielded me some good specimens of large, jet-black burying beetles and, if we hadn't frightened them and were in the mood, we would watch water shrews swimming under the crystal-clear water. One year there was a family of them, and the young ones, in playing and hunting, looked like large beads of mercury rolling rapidly through the water, but losing much of their magic once they came out onto the bank, where they reverted to grey from silver. The pool is now virtually dry and very overgrown - a pity, it was a wonderful place.

...bubbles were released if you pushed a long stick into the mud..

At Wiston Springs, we discovered that huge bubbles were released if you pushed a long stick into the mud. Mentioning this on returning to school, we learnt a number of interesting facts. The bubbles were of gases produced as leaves decomposed and the main gas is something called methane. Methane is inflammable. Methane is also produced in our gut and that is what comes out when you fart.

The next visit to Wiston Springs saw us armed with illicit matches, eager to test the truth of what we had been told. It was a still day, the gas lingered against the wall of the dam and it lit to give satisfying sheets of blue flame, flecked with orange, across the surface of the water.

The enquiring mind moved then to the more human aspects of the case. We had learnt, in chemistry, how to capture gas in a water-filled gas jar. Anyone having a bath, and feeling in the right digestive state, took with him a jam jar 'in case'. Eventually, a fart was captured in the No. 7 changing room and the bottled fart proudly shown around, but no blue flame leapt up when a match was applied. Subsequent attempts also failed. Consensus was that the fart had in fact escaped before the match could be applied.

Seeing if a fart burns.

Some genius then came up with the suggestion that ignition would be accomplished if a flame was applied at the source of emission, so to speak. Our experiments had revealed a boy who could produce gas virtually at will. He was rounded up and an audience assembled. It is clear why he vetoed a match being struck a fraction of an inch from his nether parts. It is less obvious why it was felt that a lighted candle would be all right. Anyway, all was prepared and at the word 'Now!', fart was produced and candle applied. The eldritch shriek that echoed round the school as the victim rose vertically, so startled us that no-one actually saw whether his after-burner had been alight as he ascended.

The burn was severe enough to demand Matron's attention. I would love to have heard the complicated and, no doubt, plausible story produced to explain why he was having his bum explored by one of his fellows with the aid of a lighted candle.

(Recently a friend told me about a safe method being used as a diversion amongst hands on a sheep station in the Australian outback. The 'producer' lies on his back, legs drawn up *and trousers firmly in place*. At the critical moment, a flame is brought close to the trousers. He said that a funny sound is produced. So it was when we tried it! However, this is clearly another sport in which Australia has overtaken us.)

Camp on the Downs.

The actual springs were two or three hundred yards above the pool and immediatly over them, as the Downs rose up, was a flat-topped promontory clothed with elder and box trees. A small clearing gave a safe space for a small fire, and clean water was always a few yards away down a steep little slope. It was an ideal place for our gang's 'camp' and here we came with any food we had managed to acquire, to build a cooking fire and cook using tin cans. However, our most used camp, secret to all but four or five of us, was further round the spur, quarter of a mile away in the woods. An overgrown track gave a level surface on a steep slope, from which was a clear view, once you climbed a tree, across all the fields between Mouse Lane and the Downs. Here we posted our look-outs, chopped wood with an ARP fire hatchet I had been given, lit the inevitable cooking fires, hunted (unsuccessfully) with catapults, cut and trimmed 'spears' and constructed dens and secret paths. Many happy afternoons were spent here in the summer.

The Horseshoe, with the Round Hill at the east end and Flagstaff Hill at the west end, was another regular walk and offered great scope for ambushes. A vivid recollection was finding the metal rim of a cart-wheel at the top and rolling it down the steep slope, expecting it to be stopped by a tree. Not a bit of it! Moving at enormous speed it bounded down, passed between all the trees capable of stopping it, across the track at the bottom, through a fence and, when last seen by us, was heading in the general direction of the police station in Steyning. It never occurred to us, until too late, that we might have killed someone or livestock, or damaged fences or buildings. It was all done with total absence of thought and with total absence of malice - but how stupid!

Although there was a strip of beech wood up the centre of the Horseshoe and another block of beech wood at the west end running up onto Flagstaff Hill, much of it was rather coarse grass with small patches of chalk grassland with short turf and a rich assortment of flowers. Some young hawthorn and ash were creeping out onto the grassland, which was grazed by cattle and, until 1954, by rabbits. The loss of rabbits to myxomatosis then let the trees get a better roothold and the cessation of regular cattle grazing has led to ash woodland growing up on what used to be open grassland. The spectacle we looked forward to seeing was when the dead grass was burnt off in the autumn. This swayling was done in the late afternoon and the fires continued into the early night. We watched from vantage points in the school as the fire swept round the Horseshoe and then died away.

Generally, Flagstaff Hill was the objective. Just above our tobogganing slope on the track to the top leading from Town Field up the side of the Rifle Range, was a grassed-over chalk-pit spoil mound. In those days this gave a clear view into Steyning, down the track and across to the Round Hill. It was a favourite meeting place, almost an out-door junior boarder's Parliament. Here we sat around and talked. This was The Knob, now so overgrown with ash trees as to give no proper views any more.

Just behind and beside The Knob were beech woods with some climbable trees. Although it was forbidden for anyone to be anywhere in that vicinity when the Rifle Range was in use, we took delight in running from tree to tree, sheltering behind one when there was firing, until we reached one particular straight tree, which could be climbed to a fair height keeping it between you and the butts all the time. Bullets ricocheting off the target area would whine overhead or through the trees and there was great excitement if one hit our tree. There was probably little danger to us at ground level because of the mass of trees between the targets and us, although a dying bullet might have 'bombed' you as it fell. One such actually landed in the turf between someone's legs as they sat on The Knob, but the Guardian Angels were working overtime again and no-one was ever hit. We did broaden our vocabulary again listening to military language, NCOs for the use of, if we were spotted and someone was sent to chase us off.

In the autumn, walks on the Downs and along local lanes were streaked and spotted with purple! We used the dried, hollow stems of hogweed, which grew plentifully in the area, to pepper each other - and any cars or livestock within range - with elder berries. The technique was to rake berries off the spray with your teeth until you had a reasonable mouthful, close with the enemy and rake them with automatic fire. If the stem you used was long and the fit round the berries a tight one, they could be propelled great distances with surprising velocity and accuracy. It was best not to be too ambitious over the tightness of the fit. If you were, a large berry could jam your

Gatling. Should this happen, cries of 'Play up! Play up! And play the game!' were rarely heeded by others and immediate and unconditional surrender, or precipitate flight, was well-advised.

Hogweed stems and elder berries.

The only risk in this relatively harmless form of warfare was getting items of clothing, such as white shirts, stained. Were this to happen, Matron was brought into play in disinheriting mode.

The final really regular walk was along the river Adur. The tide rising and falling gave us a good deal to watch and to explore by way of seeing how the drainage dyke sluices worked and what lived in the mud. The mud was glutinous, grey and smelly. It was also hard to get off clothes, especially from the seat of your trousers if you slipped and sat down in it - which most of us did from time to time. A few boys fished in the river for eels and dabs, and eels were one of the things we did try cooking in our camps with margarine scraped from slogs. I cannot say that the experiment was an unqualified success, but at least we tried!

The river was usually reached by going up Kings Barn Lane and then cutting across the fields on the footpath to the Iron Bridge. A walk towards Beeding, downstream, brought you to the main road at Beeding Bridge and you could go back via Bramber Museum and/or Bramber Castle.

Although we did go there occasionally, the woods in the Wappingthorn area were not very popular with us. We did wander across the fields and into them, but although there was a broad agreement between the school and local landowners that the boarders could roam so long as they kept to field edges when crops were growing, we sensed little welcome if we wandered off the track in these woods. When we went there, we kept generally to footpaths and lanes - which wasn't such fun!

Places such as Chanctonbury Ring, Cissbury and Truleigh Hill were within range, but on the edge of that for an afternoon's walk. Buses and trains were out-of-bounds and only prefects had bicycles. Once Minnie Mansell borrowed a bike, not to cycle to some distant part, but to 'have a go' down part of Newham Lane. Having reached a satisfying speed, he stopped pedalling and rose immediately in a not very graceful arc. The bike was a fixed wheel model and simply bucked him off as soon as he tried to free-wheel. Minnie did more damage to himself than to Newham Lane and had to be patched up, not for the first time, by Matron.

In 1958 I myself fell foul of a bike. By then I was a prefect and so had it legitimately. I and a fellow prefect, Rob Stephens, were oiling our bikes, changed and ready to go up to the School Field to play football. There had been heavy rain and we were under the impression that the match had been postponed, when word reached us that everyone was waiting for us. We went down Church Lane, at speed, with me leading. Suddenly, a car came round the corner from Tanyard Lane into Shooting Field. The combination of oil and water on the wheel-rims meant that the bike brakes did not work. I hit the car amidships, bounced off the roof and found myself sitting amongst a tangle of bicycles with Rob on top of me.

I had a big gash at the top of my right inside thigh where the ends of the brake lever and handlebar had done their worst. There was blood everywhere as we disentangled ourselves, persuaded the frightened garage mechanic, who had been driving, to stop saying: "There was an 'alt sign there! There was an 'alt sign there!" and go for help.

As with any good accident, a small crowd materialised from hedges and from behind gravestones to admire the wreckage, speculate on the likelihood of my losing my leg (at the least) and to debate which road *should* have had right of way at the junction (as opposed to which *did* have right of way). After a short pause there arrived the local constabulary who dispersed the spectators thus: "Who is a witness? No-one? Then bugger off!"

He then dealt briefly, but thoroughly, with me, Rob and the mechanic, as Matron, whose radar had drawn her to the spot and the local doctor, summoned by the mechanic, carried out immediate running repairs. Matron then withdrew beneath her umbrella with the policeman to discuss matters of state. At this point, the local reporter decided to interview me as I sat on the verge waiting for the ambulance. However, little escaped Matron's eye and it was a sadder and a wiser reporter who was eventually and narrowly allowed to escape arrest. My brother kindly sent me the four-line report from the *Argus*. It called me 'G. Baker' and said I was a 'border' at Steyning Grammar School - some things never change!

The ambulance turned up about three-quarters of an hour later. On its way from Shoreham to Steyning, it had happened upon a motor-bike accident by Beeding Cement works, and the motor-cyclist and his passenger had head injuries. The crew had therefore, very sensibly, dealt with that much more serious business before turning round and heading once more towards Steyning for me and Matron.

At the hospital, someone settled down to do a major piece of darning on my leg, while another put seven stitches in a cut on my thumb I had forgotten about, and removed chunks of gravel from my knuckles.   Then there was a kerfuffle outside and I was unceremoniously lifted up on the stretcher and put on a high shelf out of the way while the sewing-up party went off in a rush to cope with a youngster who had cut an artery, falling on broken glass on the beach, and beneath me the Samaritan who had compressed the artery with his thumbs between beach and hospital, had them put back into working order.

Eventually, I was taken down again from my shelf and work was resumed on my leg. In all there were thirty stitches put in and I was returned to school.   Getting me into sick-bay was an operation in itself. A stretcher does not go round right-angled bends in narrow corridors - although years later at university a team of us managed it in cave rescue practice by standing the 'patient' on his head - so the way through Long Dorm was out. This left Matron's stairs from the staff entrance hall. These are steep and twisting, but were accepted by the ambulance crew as a challenge and good training and I was not allowed to do what I wanted to do - hop up.

It was a couple of weeks before I was allowed to limp out again into the wide world and, for some time after that, had to have my dressing changed daily and a hot lanolin poultice applied. This was fine when Matron was on surgery duty, but when Nurse was on duty Matron commanded that I collect the poultice from surgery and get Pop Russell to give help, if help was needed. Help was not needed from Pop. Help might well have been needed from Nurse.

So far as I remember, Rob Stephens patched up his bike himself. Mine cost me 7s 6d to have straightened. The car had two doors and the roof dented and a door pillar bent. It also lost a hub-cap. It belonged to Mr Sykes the local dentist and I made sure not to ask for dental treatment for a good while afterwards!

We did hitch-hike, indeed at one time there was something of a craze for it. In those days there was less perceived risk than there is now and hitch-hikers were common-place. When I started work and drove regularly, I would pick up anyone, just to have someone to talk to for a while. I would not do so today! The hitch-hiking range was

Hitch-hiking.

not enormous and the furthest I managed was to Arundel with Jack Page to visit his (surprised!) mother. We only got back in time for tea by the skin of our teeth and by taking the risk of getting dropped at the end of Church Street. Then, someone managed to hitch to London and got stuck. He phoned to explain - or to try to explain - his predicament. A member of staff was sent to bring him back, so he had a few hours to prepare a good story for Johnny. I seem to think that the British Museum was included in it, but after that the craze faded, helped I believe by Johnny and other staff patrolling at irregular intervals. Hitching a lift from Johnny would have been like finding the Grim Reaper in the driving seat.

Johnny did find once, to his surprise, alarm and displeasure, a car in front of him being driven by one of his boarders, Roger Barnwell, and with another, Dai Tas, as passenger. Barny's father ran a garage, which explains his early familiarity with cars and with driving. I think that it was the extended gating following this exploit which gave the duo the time, and the incentive, to carry through the Coombe Court motor-bike business. They would have thought of roaring up The Twitten and past Holland Cottage on a bike constructed in the true

166

Colditz spirit, as a fitting gesture to make the minute they felt beyond Johnny's reach. I believe that, although they were optimistic about the length of that reach, his reaction would be to admire, privately at least, their spirit and initiative.

Chapter 10

Saturday nights and Sunday mornings (and evenings)

After tea on Saturdays, about two hours were given over to light entertainment. Every other Saturday, a film would be shown in Big School. The films were selected by the boarders from a catalogue on a show of hands. The catalogue was scrutinised by Johnny and an approved short-list was made. It was known for public pressure to gain the inclusion of a film not on the short-list, but success was rare in this respect. Even with this sift, one or two slipped through which gave half of Long Dorm nightmares!

The films were on large reels, but the reel had to be changed half way through the film - usually just as things were getting exciting. Since these films were lent out to people like us until they fell to pieces, you sometimes found jerky bits where chunks had fallen off and the film spliced together again. Once, a mistake was made by the lending library and *Whisky Galore* suddenly turned into a documentary about London's sewerage when the reels were changed. We decided to watch it - there was nothing else to do - and got the complete film free the next weekend. In the end it was a popular happening, because we had a film three Saturdays in a row - and we enjoyed the first reel of *Whisky Galore* twice!

The projector was always operated by two boys, trained for the task and adept at resolving tangles inside the apparatus and in splicing the film when ('when', mark you; not 'if') it broke.

The evening always began with a cartoon, usually a 'Tom and Jerry' and anyone walking along Church Street as the titles came up would have been startled by the shout of 'FRED!!' which went up as soon as the Director's name, Fred Quimby, appeared. Then followed the main event. Among the films which stick in my memory are: *The Wooden Horse*; *Above Us the Waves*; *Shane*; *Kind Hearts and Coronets*; *Passport to Pimlico*; *The Man in the White Suit*; *Singing in the Rain*; *Genevieve*; *Gigi*; *Whisky Galore*; *The Titfield Thunderbolt*;

168

The Mouse that Roared; *The Sound Barrier*; *On the Beach*; *Laurel and Hardy Meet the Ghost*; and *Bridge on the River Kwai*. This gives a flavour of the kinds of film favoured, but there were a good number of others whose names I have forgotten, including some Westerns in which telegraph poles could be seen in the background or aircraft vapour trails in the sky and in one of which we got the hero up to twenty-two shots from a six-shooter before he had to re-load.

On those Saturdays not graced with a film, there were usually two or three separate centres of activity. The TV room would be in use and there was a rota system, of sorts, to decide who watched the television on any particular Saturday. In Big School, the gramophone would be in operation, with records brought up by boys to supplement a basic collection of scratched seventy-eight r.p.m. records. The only song I remember clearly was the one in which the singer pleads with a wood-cutter to 'spare that tree' on the grounds that it was 'the only tree my wife can't climb' and that since it had in the past protected him, so he would now protect it. I can vouch for the fact that it was a very mixed bag, most of which was eminently forgettable. Anyone preferring to read quietly went to Room 4.

Basket-ball v the staff – a non contact sport?

169

Quite often the gym could be used for games of crab football or basket-ball - in my first year, boxing was one of the alternate Saturday's entertainments. The gym was used only if a member of staff could be persuaded to supervise and use of any of the apparatus was strictly forbidden. The staff quite often got up a team to play groups of VI Formers at basket-ball. I do not know why anyone is under the illusion that basket-ball is a non-contact sport. Our version most certainly was not. Yes, you attacked the ball, but, if an opponent got between you and it, then he was fair game. The wall-bars could be brought into play off which to cannon the ball and/or people. On one occasion when Flab Wright, Digger (who was strong and had a low centre of gravity) and Drip Walters (an ex-Coarse Rugby player) were on the opposing team, it was like trying to halt an elephant stampede with your bare hands. Bruises, strained wrists, twisted knees, bloody noses, and grazes were two a penny - on both sides.

Sundays were a completely different kettle of fish.

Midway through the morning, we assembled in Big School and were inspected by the Housemaster or Headmaster. We then trooped out of the Brotherhood Hall entrance in pairs and by year, with the column led by the first year and with a prefect walking on the road, level with the first pair. Prefects were spaced along the line, roughly one to each year. Johnny brought up the rear. The army advanced, briskly, upon the church.

Holland House took over the whole of the south aisle of the nave and there was, by the time I left, a small overflow of VI Formers into the north aisle. The first year was inserted in the back pews, just inside the door. In the rearmost pew and in the outside berth sat Johnny. In the equivalent berth in the next pew sat the prefect who had led the procession. The rest of the House was packed in, with the second year to the fore, and with the escort prefects sitting at the end of the pew, one to each year. The reason for the first year being at the back was not hard to guess. Johnny didn't get on with the vicar and had no wish whatsoever to listen to any sermon of his. Therefore, it was a short journey to make to the concept that eleven-year-olds couldn't possibly be expected to sit through a twenty minute sermon.

The facts that they were jolly well going to have to sit through a sermon that evening, and that every full school day they had to sit through seven forty-five minute periods, had nothing to do with the case (Tra-la!). It was equally clear that it would be extremely prejudicial to law, order and the smooth running of the school to have twenty small boys running about the place in the absence of the Headmaster, and, while we were at it, we might as well take a prefect along too - in case. Thus, as Eggie Bill advanced upon the pulpit, so Johnny, the first year and one grinning prefect made out of the door, leaving the rest of us to our fate. Once back at the school all pretence was dropped. Johnny went to read the paper before his lunch; the prefect went to a Common Room to do the same - or went out for a short walk; the juniors played, once they had changed out of their Sunday best.

Meanwhile, the rest of Holland House scratched its names in the varnish of the pews or found naughty bits in the prayer book or bible. Those pews had an almost complete inventory of the names of boys in Holland House from about 1948 through to about 1960. This record was lost when the new organ was installed in the early 1980s and the church spruced up for the grand opening. Until that time I took great pleasure, on the few occasions I was passing through Steyning, in going to the church and walking from pew to pew looking at the names of the people I had known and smiling at my own beetle logo. I found myself reminded of people I had forgotten and it was nice to sit there for a few minutes with the memories of eight formative years. I know that names scratched on pews could be thought of as unsightly - these were certainly no works of art! Those pews are rarely used today and the congregation, when I have gone to services there, has occupied a small part of the main nave. To me, and I suspect to others like me, those graffiti meant more than any war memorial or wall plaque. At least two of the bored boys who scratched their own memorials here are dead. It was good to remember them as fellow sufferers at the hands of Eggie Bill! I regret their obliteration, and wish I had known what was going to be done so that I could have made a photographic record. A major Holland House landmark has been lost.

We had a problem, from time to time, with the hymns. Holland House gave voice most lustily, if it knew the hymn. If it did not, it was mute or virtually so. Since we produced a good half of the sound going up unto the Lord from Steyning Church's matins service, He may have had to adjust His volume control from time to time! If we were in full flow in a hymn we all enjoyed, we could hear nothing except ourselves and occasional hoots from the organ. When at school, we sang at a brisk tempo, on the basis that to do so left us little time to fill with mischief. If we sang a Bach chorale tune we sang it *ff* and quickly. As we discovered, the Steyning Church choir and congregation sang it at a funereal pace, *pp* to *p*, with expression. On drawing breath at the end of the first verse of *O, Sacred Head sore wounded*, we failed to notice that the organ, choir and congregation were only on the second line and we set off again on our second verse. By the time we realised what was happening, it was too late and we finished our three verses triumphantly, two laps ahead of the rest, who were only then trudging to the end of their first verse.

That was one good moment. The organ itself provided others when notes got stuck, usually high-pitched ones, and the organist ploughed grimly through the hymn or psalm with what sounded like a descant drone in full fig. The organist, at the time I am thinking of, was Mr Bettany, owner of Springwells and father to a day boy a year or two younger than I was. He would advance on the errant organ and hit it to un-jam the note. At last it got too much for him and he vanished into the machinery armed with a monkey-wrench. After a good deal of clanking and muttering the noise ceased abruptly and our organist reappeared, dusty and be-cobwebbed, clutching in one hand the wrench and in the other the offending organ pipe. So far so good, but we were now minus a note and so arrived at a blank space in the melody from time to time.

A cat once gave us pleasure too. It wandered in through the open door, and at some fairly early stage in proceedings. During the General Confession and Absolution the verger stalked it, under the

The organist emerged with the offending pipe.

gaze of the back rows of the congregation. The cat was not happy about being caught and said so. For reasons best known to himself, instead of taking it to the door and ejecting it, the verger raised the lid of the font, dropped the animal in, and shut the lid. The cat's songs of fury and hatred mingled with ours of joy and love and the feline contribution to prayer was to the point, but not silent.

In the summer, Johnny sometimes arranged for the boarders to walk to one of the smaller nearby churches for matins. The three I remember going to were Coombes, St Botolphs and St Mary's church at Wiston House. We walked; Johnny came by car, sometimes sweeping up the halt and the lame with him.

On Sunday evening we had our own service in Big School, usually with a visiting preacher. For this, as with the Saturday film, the desks were moved aside and more chairs brought in and set out in rows, leaving an open aisle in the middle. When all were assembled, Johnny would sweep in, driving the visiting preacher before him. Johnny would mount the dais and lead the service. The visitor sat beside the dais to the left. The piano sat beside the dais to the right. A lectern with the Bible on it was on the left side and a prefect read the lesson, unless it was one of Johnny's favourites when he would read it. He felt that I read well and, if the preacher was an important one, or if, for some reason, Johnny wanted the lesson to be heard and to make some sort of sense, he would over-ride any rota we had and demand that I read.

A number of us had been introduced to the game of sermon cricket in which runs were scored through: repetition of the text; uttering clichés; thumping the lectern; and by any umpiring signals - four, six, wide, no-ball, leg-bye and so on. Wickets were lost to raised fingers. My father was, at that time, the Education Secretary to the British YMCA, but he was also a lay-preacher. Johnny invited him to come and embarrass me. My father knew all about our sermon cricket and was determined to keep the score down. At first he did so and it was a bit like watching Mike Atherton on a difficult wicket in a Test Match. However, he then got into the story of Bishop Talbot, who was large, at a conference in Germany in the mid-1930s at which Dr Josef Goebbells, who was small, was speaking. What he said so infuriated the Bishop that he rose, strode to the front, picked Goebbells up by the shoulders and shook him saying: "My little man! My little man! You can't believe a word of what you are saying!!" This story was accompanied by an imitation of the Bishop's actions. Eleven consecutive sixes were signalled! He found the score-sheet on the driving seat of the car when he came to drive home. This bit was circled and a note from me read: 'Not bad for an amateur!'.

Most of our preachers were pretty ordinary, but from time to time we had an exceptionally good one - or an exceptionally bad one. There was a very diffident and inarticulate young man once, who held up a card with a key word on it for each of the five sections of his sermon. The initial letter was large and clearly legible at the back. The rest of the word was writ small. After twenty minutes of muddled thought and incomprehensible conclusions he decided to recap by picking up his cards one by one in his left hand and transferring them to his right hand, where they fanned out like a hand of playing cards held facing the audience. The initial letters spelled: 'SORRY'!

Another preacher earned us all a scowl of tremendous ferocity from Johnny. He was impressing upon us that he wanted us to remember two things; just two things! This demand was emphasised by gesture, but, unfortunately, unlike Winston Churchill, he made it with the back of his hand turned to the audience. It was an audible mutter of : "And the same to you!" from the senior half of the congregation, which gave Johnny the opportunity to assume his grade one, frightening-gargoyle, expression.

This was one instance of when more people acted in unison than anyone had expected and what was meant as an aside heard only by immediate neighbours became a communally expressed and widely heard remark. The most amazing one I remember was when everybody, but everybody, sang lustily in Assembly of the shepherds washing their socks by night, and were so shocked that everyone just stopped singing and stood mute waiting for bolts to descend from on high. For someone who had been taken quite unawares by this, I thought that Johnny performed creditably, as three-hundred and fifty boys wished that the gym floor would swallow them up.

While the majority were in Assembly, the Parish Church, boarders service or evening prayers, the small number of Roman Catholics had their separate arrangements. On Sunday they went to Mass in their own Church. For Assembly they had their own short service led by one of the Roman Catholics on the staff - Jonah or Ike Williams. For evening prayers, they simply did not come into Big School, but had an extended break between first and second prep. The disadvantage to this was that they might miss announcements and the first question any Roman Catholic friends would ask you when next you met was: "Any announcements?" All other denominations mucked in with the

Church of England! At that time everyone had 'Christian names' and the enriching complication of students drawn from multi-ethnic and multi-faith backgrounds had not yet arrived in Steyning.

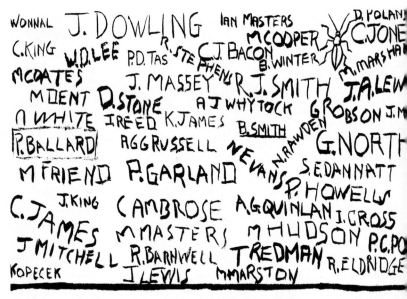

Names scratched on the pews of the south aisle.

Chapter 11

Mischief, sex and sin

School rules cannot cover all eventualities. There was no rule, for example, which stated explicitly that boys should not store high explosives on school premises.   I imagine that it was with a combination of alarm and resignation that Johnny listened to the news brought to him by Mr Sykes, the dentist. Mr Sykes's son, in company of person or persons unknown, but from the school, had found several live rounds of .303 rifle ammunition on the rifle range. His son had placed one round in a vice, applied the tip of a six-inch nail to the percussion cap and given the other end of the nail a blow with a hammer. A splinter from the metal cartridge case had skimmed the boy's temple, giving him a cut from the corner of his eye to his hair-line. (The Guardian Angels working overtime again!) Mr Sykes felt that Johnny would be interested to know that his school almost certainly contained a further round or two concealed about its person. Johnny was indeed interested and next morning descended like Attila the Hun upon Assembly.

His stirring address began with a factual account of what had happened. It went on to say that everyone should go at once to form rooms, with no diversions to lockers or other likely places; that desks would be searched; that prefects would accompany boys to their lockers so that these could be searched; boarders would, in addition, have bedside lockers and tuck boxes searched; in this process anyone with caches elsewhere of anything explosive should admit to them. Finally, that there would be an amnesty over other illicit materials such as catapults, cigarettes, matches, magazines of the kind we shouldn't have because we were too young, and alcohol.   This partially relieved a number of extremely concerned minds, but it is a safe bet that such materials vanished from the face of the school earth for a period afterwards. It was also made clear that no punitive measures would be taken against those found in possession of live ammunition. This was simply a safety operation.

The day boys' lockers yielded relatively little - a few shot-gun cartridges, some .22 and .303 rifle cartridges and a couple of aircraft cannon shells. It was in the boarders' tuck-boxes that a richer vein was discovered for us to mine. The day-boys' list of armaments was replicated in its range, but multiplied in its quantity. To it was then added: detonators; four inch and two-and-a-half inch smoke canister and high-explosive mortar bombs; signal flares; German incendiary and high-explosive aircraft bombs in a range of sizes; one anti-aircraft round; one howitzer shell; and a round which Ike Williams thought was a tank shell. This arsenal was laid out on Coombe Court lawn, since most of it had been stored in tuck-boxes there. It looked like recent photographs of IRA caches discovered by the security forces and subsequently displayed to the Press.

The search for explosives.

The British Army's Bomb Disposal Unit was based conveniently close at Horsham. It took very little time to get them to the scene, which the personnel attending viewed with considerable admiration. While a lot of it was quite harmless, unless put into vices and struck with hammer and nail, some of the aircraft bombs and high explosive mortar bombs were, in their view, too dangerous to move and should be detonated where they lay by means of controlled explosions. Now, although Coombe Court would have to be demolished at some not too distant date, Johnny had rather counted on two or three years more from it. It was explained that even a banger let off on the lawn might trigger either the collapse of the house upon itself, or a landslide into the valley, of which the building would be the prominent feature. The bombs concerned were eventually taken, with due care, to the Town Field and made safe there.

The following day, the school Assembly was told what the boarders had been told in no uncertain terms the night before. No explosives must be brought onto school premises in future. Should anyone find anything anywhere which looked even remotely like ammunition, explosives, bombs, shells or hand-grenades they were to be left exactly as they were, the spot marked and the police told and, if needs be, guided to the spot. Although Steyning itself had no harbour or beach, this applied to any naval mines discovered on beaches and 'something lingering with boiling oil in it' would await anyone trying to bring one to school. These things were dangerous and, although he did not love us much, he rather wanted to return us to our parents relatively intact and, while we were at it, although possession of guns, be they sixteen inch naval guns, army field guns, machine guns, rifles, pistols or shot guns was not explicitly forbidden by the rules, these items were not to be brought to school either. Were we clear in our minds of his views on this general topic? Yes, sir! We were, sir!

In spite of this we were allowed to buy fireworks. The general idea was that these should be donated towards a Holland House firework display in which we did our best to set the school alight. Of course, things such as bangers were bought in considerable quantity for our private uses. These included using bangers as miniature sticks of dynamite in the chalk pits, as well as grenades with which to spice up ambushes. The worst accident happened at Bramber Castle where a small group of local girls was larking about with some of the boys and a banger fell down the front of one of the girls dresses. Luckily the damage was not so bad as it well might have been. It was not an

A banger used as 'dynamite'.

accident which could be concealed from Authority and there was no attempt to escape responsibility. It was clear that no malice lay behind the incident. Indeed the victim was contributory to it and, luckily, the girl's parents understood. It was, however, a shocked and contrite group of young men who had to make their apologies and the school was, once again, read a lesson about common sense and responsibility.

The only other explosive we tinkered with was ammonium tri-iodide. This was easily made by dissolving iodine crystals in eight-eighty ammonia and then letting the sediment dry by evaporation. You could apply this in its wet state to, shall we say, a black-board duster, or scatter it across the floor of the teacher's dais. Once dry, it exploded on contact, producing a cloud of purple vapour. Pretty harmless and pretty juvenile, but it made first lessons interesting.

The deed was done by Jack Page and myself. We knew how to get hold of the complete sets of school keys and so had access to any classroom or lab. These provided the necessary apparatus and targets. It also provided the ammonia, but the iodine was kept in the poisons cupboard and only Buffer held the key to that. However, Jack and I could open it, using a school knife, and close it again, leaving it locked except for a top bolt.

We toyed with the idea of making ammonium tri-chloride, one of the most powerful chemical explosives there is and one so unstable that it explodes if touched, moved or if sunlight falls on it. It is made very easily and our idea was to assemble the necessary apparatus and chemicals in a hole in a field on the Downs. The expectation was that gas bubbles would trigger detonation, even if sunlight did not. We would set everything up, pour on the final ingredient and leg it to a very safe distance. Fortunately, we did not try it. Had it not gone off as expected, we could not have risked going back, and that would have left us in the awful position of having to tell someone what we had done in case the farmer, or anyone else, got blown up later. Common sense did prevail occasionally.

Johnny was by no means repressive, unless faced by unreasonable or dangerous activities, and would turn a Nelsonian blind eye to some activity carried out by an individual who he felt would be careful and sensible. When dormitory captain in Upper Dorm, I found that by going out of the window onto the pitched roof of Big School, you could get up to a perch between the two chimneys at the top of the Brotherhood Hall tower. You could also move over the roof of Long Dorm and, indeed, over Holland Cottage as far as The Twitten. You could get to ground level from the end of Long Dorm's roof by using Matron's fire-escape. As I have mentioned, it was possible to get close to the windows of the maids' rooms, but that roof was tiled and less safe than the slabs of the Church Street buildings. Johnny knew that I did this and made it plain that he knew by referring in jocular fashion to 'certain nocturnal mountaineering activities' - to the mystification of anyone not in on the secret. I was trusted not to break my neck, to damage the roof, to fall through his bedroom ceiling (now there *is* a vision!) or to alarm the local population. If I caused him no problems, he would cause me none either. This was a VI Former displaying the sort of individuality and adventurousness that he hoped for from his students.

There was a (usually friendly) running battle between us and boys living in the town. On one occasion, small green apples were being used as ammunition, the Church Street frontage was taking a good few hits and the Brotherhood Hall windows some shrewd blows. It is not easy to get any distance or direction throwing out of the windows and sorties from the main entrance were risky. If, however, well armed special forces got up onto the platform between the Brotherhood Hall tower chimneys, the infidel could be outgunned and demoralised because he did not know from whence the barrage came. I was a javelin thrower and could cover from beyond The Twitten in one direction to the slope running up from the High Street to the White Horse in the other. If the enemy kept out of our range they had no chance of bringing us under fire.

On another occasion I caused Long Dorm occupants, including the dormitory captain, Willie Trelawny, some concern by flicking small pieces of plaster into the middle of the dormitory from the end window. Since the window was high up, no-one thought of it as the source. There is in fact a wide strip of flat roof just outside it on which you can lie, concealed from those inside. Willie had worked out that the ceiling was not falling down, as his young charges feared, but had not arrived at a plausible source of the debris by the time that I let him in on the joke.

Those who approached him with requests to be allowed to do something out of the ordinary, usually found Johnny prepared to listen, if not always prepared to sanction the suggestion. We had heard that there was motor-bike scrambling scheduled one Saturday at an old chalk-pit at Hill Barn near Small Dole. We were uncertain how it would be viewed were we to go there without permission, so four of us went to ask about it. What was this 'scrambling'? We explained as best we could and he commented that it sounded unnecessarily noisy and dangerous, but, if we cared to get into his car, he would drive us there, come in with us, and see for himself whether this was something he was happy for boys to go to. We leapt at the offer.

The Headmaster's car was readily identifiable at distance by any boarder and, as we neared the place, figures could be seen diving for cover. We had to say we hadn't noticed anything when Johnny suggested that other boys from the school were intending to while away the afternoon in that part of Sussex. Once inside, two of us at a time had to stick to Johnny to try to steer him clear of confrontation with stray members of Holland House, while the other two, on the pretext of finding him the best vantage point, rushed round warning cap-less boys, smoking cigarettes, that their Headmaster was, even as we spoke, moving gently through the crowds, like a crocodile in a muddy river and might at any moment be upon them in a flurry of teeth and claws.

I do not think that Johnny's doubts about safety were materially allayed when we saw a competitor ride straight through the First Aid tent, breaking a first-aider's leg. I cannot pretend either that the sport was anything other than noisy. If you were after a tranquil stroll on the Downs, Hill Barn was not the place to be. We had an enjoyable time ourselves, although we had some explaining to do later, amongst boys senior to us, about loosing Johnny on them without warning and in the one place in the area they thought he would never be. I never went to watch scrambling again, so I imagine that Johnny decided it was not a good idea for boys to go there unsupervised, although I cannot remember any announcement about it. I do suspect that Johnny enjoyed himself in his own way. Quite apart from having a questioning mind which, having been made aware of something going on not previously experienced, needed to 'run and find out', he cannot have been so blind as he pretended! If we noticed panic-stricken flurries as we rounded bushes and mounds in our stately progress, he must have done so too.

There were three things high on the list of capital offences - smoking; drinking alcohol; and sex. All of these were matters of likely concern to parents and the school could not be seen to condone them. Only on one day a year were all three given qualified official sanction, and then only to VI Formers at The School Dance, to which Old Boys, staff and guests were invited. However, we were expected at the Dance to act as sophisticated young gentlemen and usually did. It was the Old Boys who were at the bottom of most of the escapades - such as picking a car up bodily (I think the car was Dave Hurry's) and putting it into the bicycle shed at the top of Burdock's Slope, from which it could be extricated only by carrying it out again or, alternatively, demolishing the bike-shed. The Old Boys were also responsible for exchanging the School Flag for a pair of panties and a bra, and so fixing the flag-pole halyard that several hours elapsed before these trophies could be brought down. The flagpole rose high above the pitched roofs of Rooms 4 and 5 and so was clearly visible from the High Street and The Twitten.

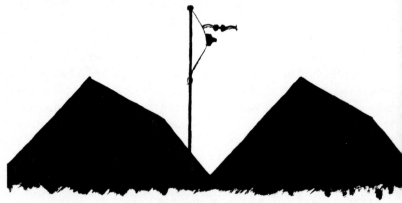

The Old Boys' replacement for the school flag after the Dance.

Many boys did smoke, and some were serious smokers. Smoking was very much a social custom amongst adults, especially men, and was something many aspired to as a sign of maturity. Cigarettes were expensive, hence the value to the impecunious of the Penny Drink Shop selling single Woodbines - themselves the cheapest cigarettes.

At the other end of the scale were Three Castles, the oval Passing Cloud, and Sobranie Black Russian. Anyone caught smoking could expect short shrift, although on one occasion Buffer Bennett kept a boy who had concealed a lighted cigarette by cupping it in his hand and putting his hand in his pocket, talking until it burned him and then said: "Oh put it out boy and don't be such a fool!" There was a distinction, though, between a boy close to you puffing away, and a faint cloud down-wind of a group standing, for example, by the gate into the Rifle Range from the Mill Field. The latter might cause a prefect to alter course in a leisurely way and head over to express the desire that those concerned shouldn't be so damned obvious - or in some cases, I am afraid, to cadge a fag! The former would be something no prefect or member of staff could overlook.

From time to time there were purges. Occasionally, the purge would be a full scale one, similar to the search for explosives. More usually, a posse of prefects would be sent forth to get everyone to turn out their pockets - and it is mind-blowing just what a junior can and does cram into his pockets. When I first experienced a purge, Matron herself walked round to look at the unholy mixture of the notionally edible, the patently inedible, and the entirely insanitary, and to remove some of the most treasured of our possessions on grounds that they were a hazard to our personal and the school's corporate health.

The primary targets of purges were cigarettes and matches. Matches by themselves were the lesser of the two evils, but if you had matches, you were assumed to have used them to light cigarettes unless you could prove innocence. Evidence of cigarettes, even if that evidence was an empty carton, was treated seriously.

So it was that, when I was about fifteen or sixteen, I was pressed to wait upon Johnny in his study to discuss with him my possession of a match box and a tin, the label on which claimed it to have held twenty Benson and Hedges cigarettes. Johnny expressed great disappointment in me. He felt also that my parents would be grieved.

It was the second time in my school career that Johnny had accused me of something unjustly. The first time had been right at the end of my first term at the school. It was just before Christmas, and I had withdrawn all my money from the School Bank - it was about ten shillings and six pence - and had spent all but the six pence on edible Christmas presents for my brother, two sisters, grandmother, and parents. Johnny saw me with this armful, inspected it, and next morning in Assembly told the school how shocked he had been to find a boy (un-named) wasting ten shillings on tuck. The sense of outrage and of being unfairly treated was immense, but I was too unsure of myself to ask to see him so that I could put things straight. I was not unsure of myself now, and was both totally innocent (I never did smoke at school) and fire-proof, since it had been my father who had given me a supply of tins and match boxes. The hinged tin was perfect for catching interesting insects sitting on leaves - nettle patches were excellent hunting grounds. You held the tin open in one hand and cautiously advanced it. Then you snapped it shut over insect and leaf and gently eased the leaf out, leaving the insect inside. Once back at school you released your capture inside a net or a container which let you inspect it and then release it or add it to your collection as you wished. I think I was probably credited mentally with nine out of ten for ingenuity and plausibility at this point. I explained that match boxes were equally useful for catching beetles on the ground, or things like wasps on windows. At this point Johnny picked the match box up and shook it. It rattled. Scowling ferociously he opened it, before I could prevent him, to expose the incriminating evidence. This flew out and made for a window, luckily a closed window, being no match, but a large, rare and cross solitary wasp captured by me with considerable difficulty from a log in Coombe Court garden in which it had been excavating a brood chamber. There followed an educational minuet for Headmaster, boy with match box and wasp. While it lasted, I lectured Johnny on the habits and merits of solitary wasps and of the extreme value to me of this particular specimen. I was then able, at last, to give a practical demonstration of how a match box ought to be used by any entomologist worth his salt, and left my

Headmaster meditating upon the richness of school life. I do not recall him again opening, or even asking me to open, any container found in my possession.

A minuet for wasp, headmaster and a boy with a matchbox

Drink rarely caused problems. It was too expensive and most of us were so unused to it that our heads span if we were given half a pint of beer. Much more made us ill, and the consensus was that drinking 'wasn't worth it'. It did get me into trouble twice and, another time, gave Matron a fright. My brother was at the bottom of it on all three occasions and he was not even at Steyning, but at Christs Hospital.

At the end of one Easter term, he brought back from school a ginger beer plant - in essence a colony of yeast. To this white sludge, you added sugar solution and powdered ginger. Everything bubbled merrily for a while and, at the prescribed moment, the liquid was poured off, lemon juice and a little more sugar added and the mix bottled. The residual sludge was divided into two, and you began the process again, this time with two ginger beer plants. After the next batch, you had four plants and so on. It produced a pleasant fizzy drink. Need I say that ginger beer plants arrived in Steyning at the start of the summer term? By half term there were a good number bubbling away. Shortly after half term, two things happened almost simultaneously. First, Matron on investigating a sticky puddle beneath a bed-side locker found the lower compartment looking like a hedgehog turned inside out. Splinters of glass were impacted in the wood from an exploding bottle. She had not had time to investigate the cause before Johnny was upon her steadying a boy. He had been pacing his lawn lost in thought, when the Sacred Turf was desecrated by a rather flushed and wobbly junior boy who addressed him in terms more familiar and jocular than those expected by a Headmaster of his junior pupils. The boy was clearly ill and, full of concern, off Johnny marched him to Matron. Services nurses have a fund of practical experience to draw on: "This boy is drunk!"

Once a sadder and a wiser boy arose from the bed in which he had been placed to sleep it off, the inquisition began. Where had he got the drink? He protested his innocence, against overwhelming odds. At this point Matron began putting two and two together and remembered exploded bottles in lockers. All right, what *had* he drunk before seeing the Headmaster on his lawn? Home-made ginger beer! *Lots* of it, because it had been a hot day. It had occurred to none of us that, in using the sugar to produce bubbles to give the ginger beer its fizz, that yeast does not generate carbon dioxide alone, but also alcohol. Not that this saved me! Johnny now took over. Where had the boy got his ginger beer plant from? Where had the boy who gave him half of his get *that* from? And so on until there, at the bottom of the pile, was me. This time I got the biology lesson from Johnny, who then, I imagine, telephoned the Headmaster of Christs Hospital, whom he knew, to suggest to him that his school had by that time probably been responsible for turning half of Britain's school children into alcoholics. Incidentally, Oswald Flecker, the Headmaster of Christs Hospital, illustrates how an incautious remark may haunt a schoolmaster. In his inaugural address to the school, he outlined their relative roles by saying: "You are the machine: I am the oil". From that moment on, 'The Oil' he remained.

Back at Steyning, ginger beer was reclassified as an explosive and added ahead of its times to the prohibitions with which I began this chapter.

Much later on in my school career, I was summoned to Johnny's study and invited to give an immediate and a full explanation of why that afternoon I had been carrying what looked like a crate of beer out of the White Hart pub by Stopham Bridge, some fifteen miles from Steyning. He had seen me with his own eyes as he drove over the bridge - a narrow one with the traffic controlled by lights. By the time he had been able to turn round and come back, breathing fire and seeking whom he might devour, I had vanished. This time I was absolutely fire-proof as well as totally innocent. I and twenty-one of my peers had been playing cricket all afternoon.

My brother, in those days, looked very like me. At Christs Hospital they had free days from time to time and those with bikes would set off, and anything in a thirty mile radius was within range. Although for much of the year the uniform of knee-britches, bright yellow socks, white shirt with 'bands' like those of a Methodist minister, and long dark blue coat with leather belt and silver buttons would make confusion with a Steyning VI Former impossible, the summer wear of grey flannels, white shirt and dark blue blazer made it very likely. I was myself brought to an abrupt halt for unwitting infringements on several occasions by Christs Hospital staff when I visited Andrew at his school. This time, he and a few friends had cycled to Stopham, hired a boat and had been provisioning the craft as Johnny passed. By the time he returned they were well down the Arun.

I do not think that I ever told Johnny, because in finding I had a cast-iron alibi, he simply let the matter drop.

The final episode involved a Christs Hospital free day too. Once again, Andrew had mounted his bike and, this time, spent the lunch hour on the beach at Shoreham and quenched his thirst while he was at it. Cycling back had been a bit tricky, and had not got off to a very good start when, under the eyes of a policeman, he had jumped onto his bike to ride away without unlocking it. There was then a moment of further confusion while he tried to remember the combination number for his lock. By the time he reached Steyning, he felt that a rest would be helpful, and, possibly, an aspirin. He knew where my bed was, and so propped his bike against Coombe Court wall, went in, lay down on my bed and went to sleep. There, a junior looking for me found him and, believing that I was unwell, went to find Matron. She was air-borne down The Twitten, but soon realised that she was faced with a reprobate from another school. An aspirin was provided and a search party sent out for me. However, there seemed nothing in any rules to prevent my offering, *in absentia*, succour to my younger brother by lending him my bed in his hour of need, and the matter was concluded without reference to either of our Headmasters.

There seemed to be an assumption that sex ceased to exist during term time. No boarder could afford to be seen talking to girls, let alone walking out with one, and savage strips were torn off you by your Housemaster, your Headmaster and anyone else in authority who happened to be about the place if you were. It was as bad, or worse, to be found 'playing with' another boy or, O Shades of Sodom and Gomorrah, in bed with another boy. No matter how Draconian the rules, not even the sternest of Johnny's decrees could prevent surging hormones affecting the school-full of adolescent males which was their target. As Simon Raven says in one of his books, there is an age when it becomes an urgent demand in boys to have contact with flesh - any flesh! The things I have mentioned happened, of course. However, having said that, I can remember only four occasions in the eight years that I was there when relationships between two boys became anything more than casual, growing-pain, comfort-stops. The main danger was an older boy imposing on a totally uncomprehending younger boy, and both staff and prefects kept a wary eye open for any signs that this was happening. It happened once to me, and, although the boy concerned took it in good part when I refused to let him get into my bed, I was frightened and confused enough to pretend to Matron to be sick, in an attempt to avoid it happening again. As I have said before, Matron was no fool and, I found myself in a different dormitory very shortly afterwards. It was not for another year or so that I realised what had prompted his suggestion and, had it been repeated then, who knows, I might well have said 'yes' and enjoyed it. By the time you arrived in the upper strata of the VI Form, if not sooner, these growing pains were largely past and the focus was girls.

Herein lay a problem. Within the school itself, there was a dearth. Although almost everyone would have loved to have gone out with

Nurse, to have done so would have meant persuading her (a pipe-dream in itself) and eluding Matron (virtually impossible). Both Glubbie and Johnny had daughters in our age-range, but the risks and complications of attempted liaisons here, blew any thoughts along those lines clean out of the water. This left one, possibly two, of the maids. In spite of their strictures when Pop Russell and I appeared like a couple of old tom cats on the roof near their bedroom windows, Pop did persuade Mary to take a walk with him up Mouse Lane where, as unkind fate disposed, Johnny saw them. The subsequent discussion between Headmaster and School Captain was carried out in private and was, probably, uncomfortable to both.

Outside the school, the field was wider. Leaving aside Slack Annie who displayed her well-painted charms more or less publicly in that part of the High Street between Church Street and Burdock's Slope, there were a lot of girls notionally available. However, we had disadvantages when it came to competition with local boys. We couldn't take the girls to the cinema, a local pub, or even into a café for a cup of tea. We couldn't invite them home to listen to records. We had little money. We vanished off the face of the earth in the holidays. We could not rely on sneaking out of school to keep assignations and if we did manage to turn up on time and in the right place, it was more than likely that the romantic tryst would end in precipitate flight when a master hove into view. Many of the local girls went to the Sec. Mod. and between them and us was a great gulf fixed. Over at Beeding Convent was a group of girls incarcerated there in term time. They were guarded by nuns, but we were able to meet, usually by accident rather than by design, and not for long. Their repertoire of dirty jokes put our meagre store to shame, and it was from one demure little girl that we acquired a hand-written set of over a hundred verses of the legendary poem *Eskimo Nell*. Beeding was, in any case, far, far outside the 'sneaking out of school for half an hour' range we worked to.

This left, in essence, the Steyning girls attending Horsham High School who, like most of us, just wanted some friendly contact with members of the opposite sex of their own age, social and academic background. We often met in small groups - it was quite uncommon to meet just one-to-one - and it really was just talk for the most part, whatever we might boast about (or think about!). All very innocent! It does explain the rustle of bushes outside the station when the afternoon train got in from Horsham, but the voice from the midst of the bush was not that of God speaking to Moses, but of boy to girl making arrangements to meet.

Meeting girls at the end of Dog Lane.

By far the most usual place for meetings was Dog Lane, in the short window of time between lights-out for the rest and the moment that prefects and other VI Formers were expected to be in bed themselves. Dog Lane is dark, it is close to the various exits from the Main School, Coombe Court garden and the other popular routes which leaked senior boys in its direction. You needed only to choose your moment crossing the High Street and you were relatively safe. The girls knew our staff by sight and, should there be a master lurking in Dog Lane itself, one of the girls would come to the High Street to warn us. Dog Lane has the advantage too of offering places where you can see down it towards the High Street and, at the same time, up to Sheep Pen Lane. You could see anyone coming your way from either of the likely sources of staff invasion and move accordingly.

Finally, there was Elsie and Doris Waters' orchard and dear Elsie and Doris themselves. They were famous music-hall stars, whose 'Gert and Daisy' dialogues were among the war-time morale-raisers (and used also by the Ministry of Food to put across helpful hints!). Their brother, Jack Warner, was a well-known actor who I associate with the police TV series *Dixon of Dock Green*. Elsie and Doris acted as look-outs for us from their house opposite the White Horse, and many were the times when one or other would suddenly appear and advise us to hop over into the orchard, because a master was heading our way. I am sure that, had there been need for it, they would have hidden us in the house or, between them, created a diversion to allow us to escape - knowing them by turning into Gert and Daisy and discussing, loudly, the member of staff concerned, his principles, morals, appearance, and so on.

Chapter 12

The Mighty Skippings

No account of Holland House in the 1950s would be complete without mentioning David Skippings. Skippings was large. Your above average VI Former in those days might be around six feet tall and weigh, perhaps, eleven stone. Skippings, in his prime, was over six feet and weighed around twenty stone. This in no way stopped him from taking a full part, and often too full a part, in the doings of the school. Many of my more astonishing anecdotes have The Mighty Skippings at their heart. The problem was that there was no holding him back, and coupled with a tremendous desire to get involved was a tendency to act first and only once it was too late, to realise the likely consequences of a particular course of action. He would also develop lines of reasoning which, while perfectly clear and logical to himself, were not so immediately apparent to others, for example, let us say, to Johnny.

As a member of Holland House there was no question of his being excused from trying to get athletics standards. To be fair, there was no lack of enthusiasm for the attempt on his part, and officials had to step in more than once to dissuade him from activities potentially damaging to himself, equipment, spectators and innocent passers by - the pole vault for instance. Even *his* optimism did not extend to any of the running events, but seeing Skippings rolling like a human avalanche down the long jump runway or attempting to defy the laws of gravity in the high jump, were among the highlights of the athletics season. The throwing events were more realistic of success, and I cannot recall a year when he did not beat the shot standard to its knees. The discus too was a likely scalp, but the javelin was attempted more in hope than in expectation. Most important, he was always there trying and was an example to any who were themselves 'athletically challenged'.

Skippings on the long jump runway.

In football, The Mighty Skippings stood four-square between the goal-posts, surging forward occasionally to overwhelm any forward rash enough to challenge him at close range.

He enjoyed swimming and was a regular member of the group travelling with Digger to give problems to the attendant at the King Alfred Baths. That gentleman was one of the few people who actually stopped Skippings from executing a project. When the imposing sight of Skippings on the top board was pointed out to him by people of a nervous disposition, his frantic whistle-blowing and urgent gestures did take effect and the threat to the pool retreated. Success was partial. A few seconds later an almighty splash, followed by a tidal wave, indicated that Skippings had got tired of climbing down ladders and had jumped from a lower board. When he and Flab Wright, who had joined us that day, were discovered by the attendant about to perform a double-act off the spring-board, he nearly sent both of them out! One at a time was sufficient of a strain on the board and the results, while not exactly graceful, were imposing.

In the gym, there were a number of activities forbidden him. As Shocker recounted to us, prohibition alone was not enough and anyone in charge had to have eyes in the back of their head. Among the activities the class was engaged in was stride-vaulting a high box using a beat-board for take-off. This was something that Skippings was not supposed to do and it was with horror that he looked round to see a human Jumbo-jet in full flow down the run-way. His shout of 'Stop' came as the beat-board was reached and take-off attempted. As Shocker said, no box could have withstood the impact, and this one was reduced to its component sections, forming an appropriate surrounding of coffin-sized pieces to a prone and groaning would-be gymnast.

Amazingly, Skippings was never badly hurt in this and comparable endeavours. The Dormer fire-drill gives another example. For obvious reasons, Skippings occupied a ground-floor dormitory, or at least one which did not involve agility in making your escape. However, rolling majestically out through the French windows of the Dormer ground floor dormitory did nothing to dim his ardour for experimentation. Thus it was that the anchor party on the rope leading from the first floor window onto Johnny's lawn was alarmed to find, framed in the window The Mighty Skippings, beating his chest and making Tarzan calls. In vain did Johnny, standing on the slab pavement below the window, shout 'No!'. Skippings launched himself forward, grabbing the rope with both hands and swinging his legs up to gain purchase on the rope. Alas! His hands were unequal to the challenge and, as the anchor team gave ground so his grip failed and he fell to earth landing with his right shoulder on the pavement and missing by inches driving his Headmaster into the ground like a tent-peg. We swore that he cracked the paving slab he fell on, but I think that it was cracked before his descent. He did indeed hurt his shoulder, but not badly.

In the dormitory, it was others who were likely to suffer most. His own bed was specially strengthened. The beds of others were not. Once, someone had made some comment to which he took mild exception. He moved across the room, jumped up and sat on the boy as he lay in bed. It was the fact that the bed was sprung, and that the legs and frame gave, which allowed the victim to live to fight another day. Once he had been revived and his stomach disentangled from his back-bone, the victim's bed became the focus of remedial work. The legs at the front bent out to the north and those at the foot to the south. The nearside of the frame described a gentle curve rather than a straight line.

I would not say that tact and sensitivity to the feelings of others ranked high among Skippings' virtues. One momentous evening the Senior Scouts, who numbered him among their members, were out on some species of field exercise which involved a group being taken in a blacked-out car, belonging to Pog Sauvain, to somewhere off the beaten track and tipped out, with maps, to locate themselves and to return to school. As ever, there were differences of opinion about where they were. Eventually, everyone except Skippings had come to a consensus over which direction to go in and did so. Quite typically, Skippings was convinced that everyone except him was out of step and so moved off confidently himself on his preferred route. As dusk fell, the main party arrived back and reported events. A search party was organised and Pog's car set forth once more.

Meanwhile, and in total ignorance of potential catastrophe headed their way, boy stood, in the welcome darkness of the Brotherhood Hall entrance from Church Street, talking to girl. Pop Russell had taken advantage of all the boarders being in prep, to meet his local girl-friend, Diana. Imagine then their horror when at twenty-nine minutes past eight, a master's car pulled up on the opposite side of the road and began to disgorge The Mighty Skippings *et al.* To slip in through the door and to bolt and lock it was quick and easy. However a locked door would never deflect Skippings for long. He began immediately to thunder upon it. Pop and Diana could hear someone walking down the Library to investigate the din and had no option but to retreat again, this time up the stairs to Big School landing, with the intention of going along Upper Corridor, down the fire escape and getting Diana out of school via the gates at the bottom of Burdock's Slope.

All this had taken but a minute from the emergence of Skippings to Pop and Diana almost, but not quite, reaching the top of the stairs to the landing. The car drew up at eight-twenty-nine. At eight-thirty I let Junior Prep out from Big School.

Glancing up to bellow the usual admonition about excessive noise, I thought my mind was going. Pop and Diana were moving through a maelstrom of boys like ships in a rough sea. In a brief second they had vanished. I groaned inwardly. This would be the main topic of conversation amongst the juniors, not just for that night, but for many nights to come. To my immense surprise, though, no-one in Coombe Court mentioned it that evening. It must have been a bit like a subliminal message flashed up on a TV screen: the appearance for a second in their midst of the School Captain and a girl. Since girls were not permitted to be in school, especially at that time of day, it could not have been a girl. On second thoughts, it was probably only the School Captain they had seen, if that, and anything else was a figment of their prep-fevered imaginations.

Pop was under no illusions about what had happened and was inclined to feel, against all reason, that I had somehow engineered things. I, for my part, suggested that, in future, he give the duty prefect some advanced warning when he proposed putting Diana through cross-country training on the school's staircases and corridors. We then sat down to speculate about what had triggered events, rising only to locate Skippings as the sole clear target for blame. Needless to say, we got no change when we did find him. In his view, everyone and everything were ganging up on him. The map was wrong; a bull he had met on his wanderings, unreasonable; the search party inept; and, finally, Pop would have saved a lot of time, trouble and nervous energy if he and Diana had stood politely aside to let him and the search party in, under the watchful gaze of Pog Sauvain!

There was then the incident of the bomb. I have already described the great purge of explosives and of Johnny's instructions about what to do if anyone found explosives in their wanderings - mark the spot and tell the police. Skippings - it would be him - *did* know where a bomb was. Being a helpful sort of chap, he went to the spot alone, and, cradling it in his bosom, carried it from the Downs, across the Town Field and into the Police Station, where he dropped it triumphantly on the desk in front of the sergeant saying cheerfully: "Here is one for you!"

Skippings <u>did</u> know where a bomb was.

Pop Russell and I were in his room, watching the world go by from the window, when we observed Skippings, flanked by two policemen and protesting vigorously, being escorted down Church Street and in at the staff entrance. Pop expressed to me the view that although we did not at that moment know what he had been up to, we soon would.

Sure enough, after some thirty minutes came a knock on the door, and a junior passed on the message: "Please, could the Head see Russell and Barker in his study now!" Here, a weary-looking Johnny outlined the chain of events culminating, once the local police had emerged from under tables, in Skippings being returned to him with the strong recommendation that he be kept under lock and key hereafter. He went on to explain that he had spent quarter of an hour trying to get Skippings to see sense, but without success: "He takes the view that he should be praised for his bravery and for saving police time by carrying a bomb all that way. Also, that if he was prepared to carry the thing for a couple of miles, why are they getting upset when he plonks it down on the desk. He feels that they acted quite unreasonably and most ungratefully. I have been unable to change these views. Perhaps you will have better luck!"

Some hope!

We move now to guns. To air-pistols to be precise. I left the school just before this incident, but got a graphic account later from Digger, who had been appointed to head the Commission of Inquiry into it.

..a specimen of local youth...

Possession of air-pistols was against Holland House rules, but two were in school at the time concerned. One was held, if not owned, by Skippings. The other by a youth named Ian Cross. On the evening in question, Skippings was leaning from a window above Church Street in the Brotherhood Hall tower. Cross was by Wykeham. Opposite the point where The Twitten joins Church Street was, and is, the Norfolk Arms and outside it stood a specimen of local youth. I do not know what processes of thought-transference were involved, but both Skippings and Cross thought it a splendid idea to loose a shot off in the general direction

of the gentleman sedately puffing on a cigarette beneath the pub sign. They did so at precisely the same time. Their target, finding himself under fire from two places, at right-angles to one another, withdrew with extreme rapidity to the shelter of the public bar and made his frightened indignation about the homicidal cowboys occupying the Grammar School plain beyond doubt to the staff of that school propping up the bar. With the aid of copious libations, they persuaded him to abandon his more extreme ideas of retribution, but, like many appeasers before them, promised a full and searching inquiry. The initial trawl of the boarders brought to light that two marksmen were involved and not the one assumed originally. Since both the boys slept in Wykeham, the lot fell on Digger, as resident master there, to disentangle the truth - or some semblance of it - from the smoke-screen of evasion, half-truth and palpable untruth on offer.

After interviewing the boys, separately and together, several times and finding himself on rapidly shifting sands as stories were modified, previously admitted actions denied and, at one point, even that any shots had been fired ("I must have pressed the trigger in fun, but I was out of ammunition!"), Digger finally broke. He told them to go away; to sort out an agreed story between themselves; and, once this was done, to return and try to sell it to him. I have omitted to mention that while Skippings was large, Cross was about half his height and a quarter of his weight.

About half-an-hour later the staircase outside Digger's flat shook and there came a thunderous knocking on his door. Opening it, he was confronted by Skippings, holding a dejected-looking Cross by the scruff of the neck in one large paw. Thrusting the victim forward, he announced: "Cross has come to confess, sir!"

Johnny used to commandeer Skippings from time to time to row him round Wiston Lake in a heavy punt. Johnny was a little deaf, something he used to his advantage when it suited him. Skippings had a voice like one of the bulls of Bashan, and the countryside for a good way round the lake was privy to their conversations. You often heard first the creak of rowlocks and the splash of oars in the water, and then a rendition of their usual party piece:

"Row harder, Slimmings, we're not going fast enough!"

"Skippings, sir! Skippings!"

"Eh, boy?"

"SKIPPINGS, sir! The name is Skippings."
"That's what I said! Row harder, Slimmings!"

Row harder Slimmings!

It was at Wiston Lake that I had my last encounter with The Mighty Skippings. The summer after I had left I was doing some study of the lake for Johnny, and Skippings was drafted in to bring surveying equipment down and to construct a large-scale map, showing local landmarks such as trees. This he did, and I keep a clear picture of the view from the rear as he bent over his theodolite amongst the reeds. I also keep in my mind a clear picture of the map, accurate in all respects bar one - it was a mirror image. If you stand on the dam looking up the lake, it turns to the left. On the map, it turned to the right. It took a long time to get the error corrected, because no matter how much it appeared to the eye to turn to the left, this must be an optical illusion since the equipment in Skippings' hands had said that it turned to the right. We did get there in the end - some trifling inversion of angles I believe. Shortly after this, Skippings found gainful employment with the Ordnance Survey.

It was during this visit to study Wiston Lake that, as I walked up Church Street one evening, I heard the brazen voice of The Mighty

Skippings belting out the tragic, and informative, rugby-coach ditty about the blacksmith's daughter, while the mothers of Steyning covered the ears of their children. The sun sank over the Sussex Weald and: 'round and round went the great big wheel! Up and down....' And there we must leave it.

Chapter 13

Parents, plays and the end of term

Four times a year, events were put on to which parents could be invited, indeed we were encouraged to invite them. These were the: School Play; Carol Service; Speech Day; and Sports Day. The first three took place in the gym and involved us in dusty burrowing under the stage to get out and line up the folding seats, on which an audience of perhaps five hundred could be sat.

The Carol Service was broadly the same in lay-out as the one traditionally broadcast from Kings College, Cambridge, although our standards of musicianship were a few pegs lower than those of the Kings College choristers. In fact, few of us could sight-read music, or indeed read it at all, and all the parts had to be learned by rote. Some people had better memories than others, and you tended to follow your neighbours. The flaw in all of this was that they, in turn, tended to follow you. The blind indeed led the blind and frequently ended up in the ditch in a heap. In spite of this, we generally found ourselves more or less note-perfect by the day itself, and put on a creditable performance. It was the only occasion that boys sang melodiously, rather than just belting everything out as loudly as possible. We even surprised ourselves at how we sounded on the tape-recording which was made for our benefit. I remember, too, one of us surprising the rest in another way. Slopey Joe brought the basses to a sudden halt to enquire who it was singing an octave lower than the rest. I do not know if Jock Axtell developed his *basso profundo*; it is a rare voice outside eastern Europe and worth training if you have it!

The School Play involved even more rehearsal than the Carol Service did and needed costumes which had to be hired and then adjusted, if needs be, to the individual actors concerned. It also needed scenery, and here the Art master came into his own and was able to show off his skills to everyone. The standards of the scenery and of the production were really pretty high. However, school plays are notoriously accident-prone and ours were no exception. Percy Coltman, who produced the plays, must have been a nervous wreck by the end of the three performances, although catastrophe generally occurred in the dress rehearsal, when the school and staff made up the vociferous and appreciative audience.

We never achieved the same giddy heights of unintended comedy as did the Islington Boys Club in a competition held at the London Central YMCA and witnessed by my father, who as Education Secretary, had helped organise it. For reasons best known to themselves, the boys had decided on an abridged and modified version of the balcony scene from *Romeo and Juliet*. The curtain went up on Juliet on the balcony: "O Romeo, Romeo! Wherefore art thou Romeo? ..... etc" in ringing Cockney tones. When Romeo should have appeared he did not. Juliet scowled and tried again, and louder: "O Romeo, Romeo! Wherefore art thou Romeo? ....." Still no Romeo, but those in front of the audience and to the far left could see an empurpled face in the wings and Romeo tugging desperately to free his cloak which had snagged something. There was a rending sound and Romeo shot across the stage ending up flat on his face beneath the balcony. Juliet then produced the normal reaction of an East End girl kept waiting for her date, hands placed on hips, a ferocious frown: "And where the bloody hell have you been?" It was someone like John Gielgud judging the competition, and YMCA staff had a good deal of trouble persuading him that he really *couldn't* give the prize to Islington, even though it might have been the funniest thing he had seen for years.

The nearest we came to these standards was in *The Merchant of Venice*. In Act 2 Scene 6, Gratiano, Salarino and Lorenzo stand below, and Jessica is supposed to appear above and throw down a casket of jewels, before joining them to elope with Lorenzo. At the crucial moment, the window remained shut. The three on stage walked up and down for a bit, and then tried again. Still no Jessica. Percy Coltman rose from his seat and went back-stage to investigate and the audience heard clearly his hysterical laughter. Jessica, having got out of her dress to change into boys clothes for this scene, couldn't find them and was scurrying about, dressed only in underpants, searching high and low for the missing garments. These were found and, after a decent interval, up went the curtain again and Gratiano and company took another run at the scene. This time Jessica did open the window and appeared - briefly. There followed a crash, Jessica vanished leaving visible only a pair of hands clinging grimly to the window frame and, as the scenery shook, her head bobbed up and down as she heaved herself up, said bits of her speech and dropped down again, eventually hurling the casket out and vanishing completely, with a second loud crash, as she landed on the wreckage of the pair of steps which should have been supporting her. She staggered out of the doorway to go off with Lorenzo to the cheers of the school.

It was *A Midsummer Night's Dream* which produced another exciting moment. The scenery was supported by scaffolding over which the electricity cables for the lighting ran. One cable was worn and, unbeknownst to the players, the scaffolding, or part of it, was live. The fairies had particularly skimpy costumes on; it was winter; and one frozen little fairy, in warming his bum on a radiator whilst holding a scaffold pole, earthed himself. The shocked, falsetto squeal that followed stays in my memory. Fortunately, he was fine and no-one else

An electrified fairy.

was electrocuted before the school's squad of amateur electricians had replaced the offending cable and checked the other wires with an unusual degree of rigour, after being addressed fluently by Percy on the need to avoid parents seeing their off-spring done summarily to death on a public stage - sentiments probably shared, or even reinforced, by Johnny.

In the summer term we held Speech Day, in which Johnny gave a 'state of the Union' address. There was one joyous occasion when he got himself stuck using the American pronunciation of the word 'laboratory' which came across to us as 'lavatory' and had us at first puzzled and then increasingly - and dangerously - amused as we saw in the mind's eye the Bog with the splendid new wooden benches, demonstration desk and plethora of new apparatus he was apparently claiming had been installed in it. The custom was that the visiting dignitary then gave us a short speech, in which some topic of interest to him was touched upon and the school somehow brought into the thesis to have praise lavished upon it. Assorted prizes were then handed over to undeserving boys. The majority of prizes were books and, because the real ones chosen by prize-winners had not arrived by then, Johnny's own bookshelves were pillaged of impressive and not too ancient tomes, which you handed back to him after the ceremony. Next in the firing line was a response to the dignitary by a School Governor. This was a light-hearted piece designed to raise a few laughs.

This concluded the formal proceedings and we went, with parents if they had come along, to look at the exhibitions. Any subject that could be 'exhibited' was. Art, woodwork and any of the sciences were the usual suspects. To these were added exhibits by assorted clubs and societies and demonstrations by, for example, the Morris Dancers. The Gym Club put on the most spectacular display, which was, weather permitting, on Wykeham lawn. Here it was customary for Digger to appear in the middle of proceedings, complete with gown, hood and mortar board, a chair in one hand and a newspaper in the other. He would stroll out onto the lawn apparently oblivious to the crowd and the gymnasts and settle down to read his paper while boys, coming from all directions, vaulted over him. After a while he would look at his watch, fold up his paper, pick up the chair and stroll back into Wykeham.

One year, Percy Coltman wrote a play to be performed out-of-doors beneath the massive and ancient mulberry. As I remember it, the play was about a present-day school-boy, played by Yan Masters, who was shown by the spirit of the tree what it had seen in its life-time. He could talk with the various characters from different times past. In this play, I was the Devil and tricked out in a bright red furry suit, with horns and a pointed tail - I do not think I was allowed a trident! This is not to suggest that the Devil had at any time been a resident of Steyning - although, for all I know, he may have been. Yan had been taught a spell which would summon up the Devil and tried it out - at which point I dropped out of the tree, causing much consternation and stimulating the rapid tuition of Yan in exorcism (in Latin!), the end product being my running away, to the applause of the multitude. At least, that was the original idea. The fly in the ointment was the tree itself. Having stood majestically for hundreds of years, it collapsed in a spectacular tangle of enormous branches a day before the performance. There being no tree left to leap from I entered, at top speed, round the end of Wykeham where I had been concealed,

The devil in the coke shed.

208

appropriately enough, in the coke shed, arriving puffing and panting on the lawn to menace Yan, frighten the ladies and to be driven with Latin oaths, still breathless, into the ruins of the tree, where I lay concealed from view until the play ended.

Sports Day, also a summer term event, normally coincided with the Derby. Since many of the parents' minds, and those of the staff too, seemed as much focussed on the Epsom Downs as on the Steyning Grammar School sports field, the results of the Derby were announced as soon as they were known. The standard of athletics was high for a small school, but my impression was always that parents took but a passing interest in the events, even when their own sons were in action!

For boarders, any of these four ceremonial occasions gave the opportunity to show parents and siblings the sights of the school, the horrors of your dormitory, to point out the living legends among staff and boys, to show off generally, to introduce friends and, most important of all, get taken out to have tea in one of the town's cafés. This treat, to which you might invite a friend whose parents had not been able to come (as a shrewd investment against the time when the boot was on the other foot!), had to be timed so that it was over before school tea was served. It will be appreciated, from an earlier chapter, that putting away two teas one after the other would present no difficulty, but that missing school tea would be tragic, especially if you had been an active participant in the notionally main attraction of the day.

At the end of the Christmas term, the boarders put on a revue in the gym, taking advantage of the fact that the curtains were still up from the School Play. Small groups of boys got together to write and perform one act plays, turns of some kind, or to organise entertainments such as charades. Some of the items were in fact witty and well done. The majority were probably more fun to perform than to watch. Once, the limits of good taste were exceeded and the performers cast into outer darkness and commanded to stand outside the Headmaster's study until he got bored enough to come and deal with them. In my first term, a group of boys from Wykeham persuaded Digger to be a Roman emperor in a playlet which, I think, was in Latin, or something akin to it. It was an introduction to Digger's traditional contribution of a comic turn to the revue. However, perhaps the most extended comic turn I have ever seen was something organised by Penny Craig. He had about a dozen volunteers conscripted from among the staff and a mixed age set of boys. These were put in purdah in the changing room. The audience was shown a card on which was written the subject of a mime, and the first of the volunteers brought in to sit on the stage and watch. I remember two subjects clearly. One was grooming a horse, something that Penny was used to doing, but which mystified his first victim completely. The observer then brought in the second volunteer and performed to him what he could remember of the mime he had seen. And so it went on to the final mime, often wildly different from the original, after which the last observer had to guess the subject. With Digger involved half-way through proceedings obfuscation was inevitable, since he would add misleading ornamentation of his own. I think that the horse ended up as a carpet being beaten. Changing a baby's nappy was a masterpiece of accident and invention. First, Digger, instead of putting the dirty nappy in a pail to be washed, put the baby into the bucket instead, and had to retrieve it once he realised that he was about to wash and powder a dirty nappy. Then Flab Wright, who guessed what the mime in fact was about, put the baby on a chair while he got the powder and a clean nappy and, on returning to the chair, sat on the baby. The shrieks of glee from the audience alerted him to what he had done. Leaping to his feet, simulating horror, he picked up the flattened baby, patted it back into shape, and continued the nappy-changing. This threw the junior boy who had been his observer, and after a few more downward spirals in the plot, we ended up with 'unpacking a trunk' as the final observer's guess.

In addition to these special events, the end of term brought a relaxation of the normal grind of class work, or at least it did so where the majority of the staff were concerned. The last few days would see Buffer perhaps demonstrating the chemistry underlying certain

210

conjuring tricks; Arthur Lee telling us about some of the more scandalous goings on involving past crowned heads of Europe; Jonah venturing a mathematical joke by enquiring why a figure he had drawn on the board was like a dead parrot: "Because it is a polygon, boy! A polygon!"; Keith Sorrell inventing appropriate nick-names for us in French: "I am calling you 'Bêcheur', Dugnolle, because Dugnolle dug-an-hole".

Others might tell you to bring a book to read, or divide the class into teams to compete in word games. The ones with a fund of good anecdotes could be persuaded to recount them. The only people with cause for complaint were those who were leaving school after taking 'O' or 'A' Level exams. There was no question of them being allowed to go home after their exams. Oh no! There was plenty to be done about the school, especially after Johnny had decided that the coating of black material over the timbers of the Church Street facade should be removed in the interests of their conservation! Several year's-worth of 'A' Level leavers chipped away with school knives and wire brushes. Perhaps not the best way to end your school career, but a good deal cheaper than contractors!

There was relaxation in the dormitories of Holland House as well as in the classroom. This was a time when pillow-fights and raids on other dormitories - even raids on other buildings, although this was uncommon - were, if not sanctioned officially, never-the-less often found prefects and staff caught up in the action. The only person you really had to be wary of was Matron and then only if you burst a pillow. The pillow fights, with their blizzard of

Chipping the front of the school.

211

feathers, seen on films were not a good idea here if you valued your skin.

There might be dormitory feasts too. After agreement had been reached with the dormitory captain, plans were laid about what was needed and who would try to get what. Since pocket money could not be hoarded (you were not allowed to have more than a shilling in your pockets overnight), planning was needed so that items which could stand being stored for a week or so were bought first and perishables brought in at the last moment. Many dormitories had 'secret' hidey-holes, usually under the floor-boards. There was one such in Upper Dorm; a short length of floor-board with the nails sawn off level with the underside and with a knot hole into which you could hook a finger to lift it. It was as dormitory captain of Upper Dorm that I was made aware that these secret caches were (surprise, surprise), not secret from Matron. She either had a superb sense of radar to locate them, or, quite likely, had personally supervised their construction using one of the caretakers as the labour force, in the expectation that we would find them eventually, and use them. On her rounds she could inspect them in the way she did the jam cupboard. Anyway, she cornered me and instructed me that pieces of cheese were not to be hoarded, because they went mouldy - and I was shown the proof of that in the form of cheese which she had removed from our hoard. She also advised, resignedly, that chocolate should be stored in a tin, lest it be eaten by mice, and commented that she thought it would be asking too much for me to make sure we all cleaned our teeth after we had finished. It *was* asking too much!

I never heard of anyone suffering from food-poisoning after a midnight feast though, in spite of Matron's efforts, there were some pretty dodgy offerings, like week-old sausage rolls. The main enjoyment was in the planning, the concealment, the secrecy, and the anticipation, rather than in the consumption of the wildly incompatible and doubtfully edible assortment of odds and ends we assembled.

The real signal that the end of term was upon us was the announcement that we were to go to the trunk room and take our trunks to the dormitories and put them under our beds. For some evenings thereafter, we were hauled out of prep in small groups to collect our piles of clothes from Matron and Nurse and take them back to the dormitories to pack. We had to do this ourselves, with the result that a trunk looking only half full if packed by your mother, now needed a couple of friends to sit on it to get it locked. Those whose trunks went by train, stacked them on Big School landing, labelled carefully with their destinations. Those whose parents were collecting them by car, took their luggage into Church Street on the last morning, and stood there in eager anticipation of the arrival of parent(s) and transport. All of this needed help from friends. Those trunks were heavy.

Then cars began to arrive, parents were greeted politely and usually rather distantly under the gaze of your peers - after all a chap didn't want to lose dignity and face by getting kissed by Mummy, however much he craved it. Luggage was loaded and goodbyes said to any of your friends still left uncollected. The cars were a mixed bag and ranged from ones like our battered old Austin, exchanged eventually for an A40 van, to Lady Trelawny's limousine or, most notable of all, Admiral Sturdee's bright yellow, open topped Rolls Royce (circa 1930?) which sailed immaculately along Church Street, the envy of all.

Because of her commitments at home, it was often not until late morning that my mother would arrive for me. This meant that I was last to be collected. It got lonely waiting there, sitting on your trunk, and although I loved the holidays, I could almost - but not quite - have wished everyone back again to start another term.

It got lonely waiting.

Chapter 14

Johnny

Since Johnny was the only Headmaster we had, we took it for granted that all Headmasters were cast in that mould. We also took it for granted that he was privileged to do whatever he wanted, however strange this might have seemed at the time. Practising fly-fishing on his lawn, for example. This did produce a couple of good moments. Once, Joe Luker, hurrying up the steps by Dormer, saw an interesting blue-striped insect land on the grass at the edge of the lawn and was taking a specimen tin out of his pocket to catch it when he found it whisked away, indignantly, by Johnny standing across the lawn. Then, a new boy knocked anxiously on the staff-room door one day and asked a highly amused Shocker, who opened it, for advice and help, since the Headmaster clearly was ill and was standing on his lawn, in the snow, fishing in a puddle on the gravel path by the playground boundary.

Fishing in a puddle.

Anyway, no-one among the boys questioned our Headmaster's philosophy, or thought to enquire what his targets were for the school and its students. Johnny just 'was'. We knew that he had been at the school since before we were born, but knew nothing of where he had come from, what he had done, and why. I still know little, but have the advantage now of forty years reflection and some illuminating chats with his widow, Jean. This short chapter is a mix of fact and pure speculation on my part. The speculation gives a personal viewpoint. It is how it seems now to me. I know that not all my contemporaries will share my views, but hope that they will forgive me for indulging them.

The first and important point to grasp is that Johnny was not a formally trained teacher with a baggage of educational theory, and that he arrived in Steyning by accident rather than by design. He had been head-hunted from Oxford to join the foundation staff of a university college to be set up at Accra in what was then called the Gold Coast, to be known as Achimota College. After some time he became more interested in the remoter parts of the colony, where distances were calculated in the number of days it took walking them through the bush. He changed to working with the Government Anthropologist and went back to Oxford to read for the Anthropology Dipiloma.

In due course this work was wound up and he was back in England, jointly writing a text book *Common Errors in Gold Coast English*, but otherwise with no fixed plans.

He then got a message from another member of the Achimota team, Arthur Bolton, to say that he had landed the job of Headmaster at a tin-pot little Grammar School in Sussex and would Johnny be able to help out for a few weeks on a temporary basis. This he did, his quarters being a corner cubicle in Long Dorm. When, the following year, an offer was made to make the post a permanent one, he accepted, on condition that he was given proper accommodation. He moved into a ground floor bed-sit in Dormer which gave a comfortable base from which to follow country pursuits and a full social life outside school. During the holidays he would go skiing, sailing, engage in other sports and visit the south of France. This lasted for eight years until his marriage.

As the school began to develop and lose its 'tin-pot' image, there came the war. It was not known until long afterwards that he was a member of the Wiston Patrol of the 'Secret Army', specially selected and trained members of the Home Guard in the southern counties, whose job was as guerrillas, should there be a German invasion, impeding the enemy to buy time for Government to make its dispositions and strengthen defences. The hope was that they might buy as much as a week of time. This was their own life-expectancy, should an invasion take place. Each Patrol had its secret headquarters and arms dumps, and knew its area intimately, moving about it by day and night. The only time I ever had an inkling that Johnny's war had a bit more to it than that of the Home Guards I had seen on the Staffordshire/Derbyshire border, where my family lived in the war, was when he recounted blowing up a rookery in a local wood, slicing the tops off the trees with high explosive. (Farmers had too many rooks and London restaurants were eager for them as ingredients for 'game pie'.) It sounded a bit well-armed and savage for the average Home Guard unit! Only thirty years later, were the official documents on those special units released, and books published on the subject.

A bit savage for a Home Guard unit!

216

Johnny's enquiring mind and interest in anthropology led him to turn his hand to many of the tasks he saw performed by workers in the fields and woods around Steyning and if he told you how or why a particular job was done, it was a fair bet that he had direct experience to draw on. He also read widely and with enthusiasm.

By the time in 1944 when he became Headmaster, the school had thus acquired a man who was relatively untainted with current educational dogma; who took an anthropologist's objective and enquiring approach to human behaviour and community functioning; who knew the countryside around with an intimacy few could match; who could keep his counsel; and who was something of a polymath.

With meagre resources, it must have been difficult expanding the school in terms of numbers, and finding the room to put everybody. Books and other equipment were in short supply and, for many items, rationing was in force into the 1950s, which added to problems. With people being de-mobbed from the Armed Forces there was, however, a growing pool of teachers to choose from to replace those retiring and to supplement those remaining. Looking back at the changes which took place between 1951, when I first arrived, and 1968, when the Grammar School merged with the Secondary Modern and expanded to its present size, there seems to be a steady progression, under which must have lain grim determination. It cannot have been very easy.

I know that Johnny took pride and pleasure in his students doing well academically. He was, I know, very pleased by the number of boys in my year who got university places, particularly at Oxford where he had studied. He was equally pleased at high achievement in non-academic fields - Chris Carter running in the Tokyo Olympics, for example. I think that these were cherries on his cake. I feel now, that he hoped that, as well as getting a good 'standard' education, his boys would acquire at the school a good breadth of knowledge and experience and the self-confidence to express themselves, try new things and take unconventional approaches. With the day boys, he was restricted. The boarders were in the school all the time, and looking back over what I have written, it seems to me that we were encouraged to develop our individuality, albeit within certain bounds drawn usually to make sure we did not give other people - including our peers - unnecessary problems, and to make sure that we did not kill ourselves. The rules and regulations were no worse than those applying throughout Britain's schools then and as society's values, understanding and perceptions changed, so did the rules and the sanctions - the quite rapid decline in flogging for example.

During 1957-59 I was in correspondence with a geologist who was a retired teacher from another Sussex Grammar School. He helped me with advice and contacts for a geological thesis I was writing to try to gain a special open scholarship to Oxford or Cambridge. I have kept some of his letters, two of which have a bearing here. The first reads, in part:

'29-10-58

Dear Barker,

I had an opportunity to get to Steyning: so delivered your fossils on Saturday.

I thought the boys I interrogated very courteous, intelligent and friendly.

It was so nice - because so rare - to see boarders (presumably) tidy and civilized. There are many other samples!

Perhaps it is unfair and unimaginative so to quench the yearning spirit of ebullient youth?

But there it is; teachers have that as a chief objective; parents approve, and eventually youth submits - I think?'

Yes, we *were* asked to be courteous and friendly. Youth did have to submit, but only to a degree, and, beneath the tranquil surface of conformity, these pages show a good deal going on. I feel Johnny approved of this mix of friendly, courteous conformity with individuality.

The second, of which I give a brief extract, was written four months later:

> 'One school I know encourages pub-crawling for prefects on the grounds that it makes men of them. The Head is a bachelor, a scholar and also had a frustrated adolescence. He goes with them.
>
> There ought to be a twelve months training in school management for Headmasters before confirmation of appointment.
>
> I hear occasionally very high reports of your school and its future. It is getting known. It has a character and a tone.'

How pleased Johnny would have been to have seen that tribute from a seasoned professional. Arthur Gunner was very sparing with his praise and scathing in much of his comment about schools and their management at the time. Here, therefore, is praise indeed from someone who knew about educating boys.

I would agree that the Steyning Grammar School of the 1950s had character and a tone. To the boarders of Holland House, this was due in part to the staff, led by Johnny. It was due in part to the eccentricities of the buildings housing us - no-one could have invented Coombe Court! It was due to encouraging us to develop our interests where possible; in insisting that we kept fit; and in sending us out to explore and to use the countryside around Steyning. We developed influenced by a broad spectrum of experience which meant that, rather than being a production line for specialists, the school sent out at the end of their time there young men who were all-rounders.

I am, perhaps, reading too much into the choice of the Lesson read in the last Assembly of each term, a lot of schools use it, but I know that Johnny was fond of it as he read it himself. Possibly it was the relief of being free of us for a few weeks which made it a favourite! In it the teacher is seen as a guide and someone who helps you find the truth. It also hints that there is more to life than books and study.

> '..... And moreover, because the preacher was wise, he still taught the people knowledge; yea, he gave good heed and sought out, and set in order many proverbs.
>
> The preacher sought to find out acceptable words: and that which was written was upright, even words of truth.
>
> The words of the wise are as goads, and as nails fastened by the masters of assemblies, which are given from one shepherd.
>
> And further, by these, my son, be admonished: of making many books there is no end; and much study is a weariness of the flesh.'

At a personal level, I was encouraged to do the unconventional. My interest in insects, stemming from collecting beetles, helped me enormously in my 'A' and 'S' Level Zoology. Collecting fossils and studying the geology of the Weald as best I could, led directly to my winning a Trevelyan Scholarship to Oxford. This was itself an unconventional scholarship since it was awarded on the basis of a sustained piece of personal research, rather than on any set written papers. The badger watching attempts I was allowed to make, got me into research into badger autecology when at University, continued after I began to work for the Nature Conservancy. This work was helped, in turn, by Eddie Collins from Bramber Museum who built special recording apparatus with me. Work begun through the school Natural History Society led to annual scientific work-camps on Old Winchester Hill National Nature Reserve in Hampshire, and this work resulted in my getting my job. None of this was to do with conventional classroom education. All of it though was encouraged by the school.

What else? As well as in my main subjects, zoology and botany, the school gave me interests in archaeology and more recent history - especially social history. It helped develop a knowledge and appreciation of literature. It made me fit, and gave me a love of sports. It encouraged me to look at the countryside and the human activities going on in it, objectively; also to find my way about in it safely and to live off the land if needs be. I learnt to ask questions and not to accept that something was so just because a text-book - or a newspaper - said that it was. I learnt also to accept responsibility and to work constructively as part of a team. The common courtesies we had to practice, have stood me in good stead throughout my life - they cost little and you get a lot in return. I could go on, but even this list begins to add up to the questing, questioning all-rounder that I think, although I do not know, was Johnny's objective.

I cannot be sure, because he seemed to stand always that one pace back, observing, occasionally intervening, but hoping that we would use constructively the education that we were getting to develop for ourselves our individual personalities and to set and achieve our own goals. From our perspective we saw the mask of the Headmaster that he wore and rarely met the man behind it. When you did, it was heart-warming.

Chanctonbury Ring in April during the 1950's as seen from Winston Lake. From a photo by John Scragg.

Epilogue

At the end of July 1959, the curtain fell on the play begun in September 1951. After eight years of being a student, I was suddenly an Old Boy. The passage of a few minutes transformed me from the all-powerful Holland House Captain into - nothing? Well, no! Far from it in fact, because although it meant moving on and starting again I was by no means doing so as a 'nothing'.

I have probably given a false impression. Memory is selective, and I have left out a lot of the routine, the chores, the mental struggles in class and the near despair generated by some prep assignments or exams. Prefects and staff could - to your mind at least - be unjust. Friends did let you down, and young people can be very cruel to one another - they can also be unexpectedly understanding and kind. Heart-rending home-sickness could strike without warning, triggered by some unpleasant experience or something in a letter from home.

The first couple of years were the most difficult, but the tide began then to turn as you grew up physically and mentally and began, as it were, to look around you rather more at the opportunities you were being offered than at the difficulties of school life. The higher in the school you rose, the pleasanter life became for most of us. It is the same in every boarding school in which the ages of the students range from ten or eleven to nineteen years!

I arrived at Steyning by car, accompanied by my mother and quantities of luggage. I left by train with one suitcase full of essential clothes. The heavy luggage was in store with a family friend. At this time, my parents lived in Geneva and I was heading there that evening by train from London. I sat so that I could look back towards the Downs as the Steyning Stinker chugged along. It had been a *good* eight years and, of course, I would go back.

At first, I went back quite often, and boys kept in touch by letter. Some of us met each year on Old Winchester Hill too. Gradually, other things took over, and my career kept me away. Then in the late 1980s and early 1990s, as my parents became old and had to go into a nursing home, the mental and emotional pressures built up, and I looked for places where I could go to re-charge my batteries (to hide?). Steyning and the Downs were ideal. It took some time to unwind, but it says something about what the place meant to me.

During those difficult years I once had a vivid dream which remains with me. I shudder to think what a psychologist would make of it - it probably shows a basic insecurity! It is this: I was walking up Flagstaff Hill and sat down on the grass on The Knob (wonderful things dreams; I wasn't even out of breath!). As I looked across the Horseshoe, a group of boys came running and tumbling down the bank behind The Knob. They were boys I had been at school with. As they moved away, still laughing and running, one came towards me, looking at me with a slight frown and he *was* me! He just looked, and then reached out a hand, touched mine and then turned to run after his friends.

...reached out a hand, and touched mine...

I wonder what I made of myself, nearly fifty years on!

Looking back across those years I find myself still in tune with the young person that I think I was. Having now unpacked the knapsack of memories I have unwittingly carried through life, I am rather pleased to discover how much those eight years have helped me. I am interested to find how much small grievances have stuck - being given three whacks by Jonah just for blowing a feather into the air after lights-out; being suspected of spending ten shillings on tuck for myself, when it was presents for my family; remembering that Rob Smith has never repaid the half-a-crown I lent him in about 1957. The heart-jerking small landmarks I have mentioned and, in addition, the evocative sounds - the distinctive chime of the Old Market House clock; the whirr of the electric milk float in the early morning (now minus the rattle of glass bottles in metal crates, but otherwise exactly the same) - have travelled with me too. Running a hand along the beech tree branch where a cheerful imp once swung up to do a hand-stand press-up, giving me a friendly grin as he jumped down, was like reaching out to touch the past, as, in my dream, my past reached out to touch me.

Above all, though, it is the humour and fun which have endured and I still smile at the memory of Stinge Smith who, getting fed up filling in his tenth application for a university - Name; School address; Home address; Date of birth; Sex; Religion; and so on - wrote 'Yes please' in the 'sex' box. That university was the only one to offer him a place!

Standing with memories by 'Kopie's tree'

224